Over the past 15 years at the Hunt-Wesson Kitchens, we've developed hundreds of wonderful tomato sauce recipes we want to share with you. So we've taken our old favorites, retested and updated them, and combined them with our very new favorites to bring you over 200 of the best-tasting tomato sauce recipes you'll ever find. Whether you want to make an easy lasagne or the real thing; whether you want to make a ten-minute spaghetti sauce or one that simmers all day; whether you want to serve a simple family meal or create a fabulous feast for forty, you'll find exactly the recipe you need right here. We've also included some very helpful cooking tips. And, in some chapters, we've given you menu and serving suggestions.
Then, to help familiarize yourself with the incoming metric system, we've listed the metric measures for each recipe. And for those of you who enjoy microwave or slow cookery, we've flagged those recipes that are adaptable. And, lastly, we've included a substitution guide so that you can conveniently substitute one tomato product for another.

Cooking with tomato sauce is easy, economical, adventuresome, and fun, as you'll soon discover with this cookbook. We've loved compiling it for you, and sincerely hope you'll love using it for many years to come.

The Home Economists
of the
® Hunt-Wesson
Kitchens

Hunt's Complete Tomato Sauce Cookbook

Hunt-Wesson Foods, Inc.
Fullerton, California 92634

Table of Contents

4

Hunt's All-Time Favorites

Over the past fifteen years,
we've been asked for certain recipes
time after time. So we've taken all
these favorites, retested them and updated them
to take advantage of today's convenience
foods and new cooking methods, and combined
them into one wonderful chapter.

And here they are—twenty-one fantastic
recipes that are guaranteed
to become fast favorites with
your family as well.

Opposite: Hunt's Quick Spaghetti Sauce

HUNT'S QUICK SPAGHETTI SAUCE
Tastes like it simmered all day

225 g	½ lb. ground beef
	3 (8-oz./226 g) cans Hunt's Tomato Sauce
125 ml	½ cup water
	1 (2-oz./56 g) can sliced mushrooms, drained
30 ml	2 Tablesp. minced onion flakes
8 ml	1½ teasp. brown sugar, packed
4 ml	¾ teasp. oregano
3 ml	½ teasp. basil
3 ml	½ teasp. garlic salt
.5 ml	⅛ teasp. marjoram
340 g	12 ozs. spaghetti, cooked and drained

Sauté ground beef in skillet; drain fat. Add remaining ingredients, *except* spaghetti. Heat to boiling. Simmer 10 minutes. Stir occasionally. Serve over hot cooked spaghetti. Makes 4 servings.

HUNT'S VERY SPECIAL SPICE CAKE
Stays marvelously moist for days

750 ml	3 cups sifted flour
375 ml	1½ cups sugar
8 ml	1½ teasp. baking powder
8 ml	1½ teasp. cinnamon
4 ml	¾ teasp. nutmeg
4 ml	¾ teasp. cloves
4 ml	¾ teasp. allspice
4 ml	¾ teasp. salt
	1 (8-oz./226 g) can Hunt's Tomato Sauce
8 ml	1½ teasp. baking soda
	2 eggs, beaten
180 ml	¾ cup pure vegetable oil
250 ml	1 cup chopped nuts
375 ml	1½ cups golden raisins
125 ml	½ cup orange or pineapple juice

In large mixing bowl, combine flour, sugar, baking powder, spices and salt. Thoroughly mix Hunt's Sauce and soda in small bowl; add to flour mixture. Stir in eggs, oil, nuts, raisins and fruit juice; mix well. Pour into greased 10-inch (25 cm) bundt or tube pan. Bake at 350° (175°C) 45 to 55 minutes. Cool in pan 15 minutes before turning out on serving plate. Dust top with powdered sugar. Makes one 10-inch (25 cm) cake.

Opposite: Hunt's Very Special Spice Cake

HUNGARIAN POT ROAST
Excellent over hot cooked noodles or rice

1400 g	1	(3 to 4-lb.) lean chuck or rump roast
8 ml	1½	teasp. paprika
10 ml	2	teasp. salt
1 ml	¼	teasp. pepper
30 ml	2	Tablesp. pure vegetable oil
125 ml	½	cup water
	1	bay leaf
	8	to 10 small whole white onions
	8	small carrots, pared
	2	(8-oz./226 g) cans Hunt's Tomato Sauce with Mushrooms
	1	clove garlic, minced
3 ml	½	teasp. onion salt
30 ml	2	Tablesp. minced parsley
250 ml	1	cup sour cream (optional)

Trim excess fat from meat. Sprinkle with paprika, salt and pepper. Brown in oil in Dutch oven over medium heat. Add water and bay leaf; simmer, covered, 2 hours or until meat is almost tender. Skim off fat. Place onions and carrots around meat. Add Hunt's Sauce, garlic and onion salt. Cover; simmer 50 to 60 minutes longer until meat and vegetables are tender. Add parsley. Just before serving, remove from heat and gradually stir in sour cream, if desired. Makes 6 to 8 servings.

STUFFED GREEN PEPPERS
An easy, new way to cook an old-time favorite

	4	medium green peppers
450 g	1	lb. lean ground beef
500 ml	2	cups cooked rice
60 ml	¼	cup chopped onion
8 ml	1½	teasp. salt
.5 ml	⅛	teasp. pepper
	2	(8-oz./226 g) or 1 (15-oz./425 g) can Hunt's Tomato Sauce
250 ml	1	cup shredded Cheddar cheese

Wash and halve green peppers lengthwise; remove seeds. Lightly mix beef, rice, onion, salt, pepper and ½ cup (125 ml) Hunt's Sauce. Pile into pepper halves, arrange in shallow baking dish. Pour *remaining* Hunt's Sauce over peppers. Cover and bake at 350° (175°C) 45 minutes. Remove cover; top each pepper with cheese; bake 15 minutes longer. Makes 4 to 6 servings.

ONE-PAN CHOPS AND RICE
A delicious, flavorful, trouble-free dish

	4 chops (pork, lamb or veal) ½-inch (1 cm) thick
	Salt and pepper
30 ml	2 Tablesp. pure vegetable oil
	1 onion, chopped
125 ml	½ cup sliced celery
375 ml	1½ cups water
30 ml	2 Tablesp. sugar
8 ml	1½ teasp. salt
	1 (15-oz./425 g) can Hunt's Tomato Sauce with Tomato Bits
250 ml	1 cup uncooked rice
	1 (10-oz./283 g) pkg. frozen peas, thawed

Sprinkle chops with salt and pepper; brown in oil in 10-inch (25 cm) skillet. Remove chops. Brown onion and celery in skillet drippings; add water, sugar, salt and *1 cup* (250 ml) Hunt's Sauce. Bring to boil. Stir in rice. Place chops in rice mixture; cover tightly; simmer 30 minutes. Add peas; pour on *remaining* Hunt's Sauce. Cover; simmer 15 minutes longer. Makes 4 servings.

EASY-DOES-IT SWISS STEAK
You don't even need to brown the meat first

45 ml	3 Tablesp. pure vegetable oil
900 g	2 lbs. round steak 1-inch (3 cm) thick
60 ml	¼ cup flour
	1 envelope dry onion soup mix
	1 (8-oz./226 g) can Hunt's Tomato Sauce
125 ml	½ cup water

Pour oil in 7½- x 12- x 1½-inch (18 x 30 x 4 cm) baking dish. Place in oven at 400° (205°C). While dish and oil heat, trim steak and pound *2 tablespoons* (30 ml) flour into *each* side. Place in heated baking dish; turn to coat both sides. Sprinkle on soup mix. Pour Hunt's Sauce mixed with water over all. Cover tightly. *Reduce oven temperature to 325°* (165°C). Bake 2½ to 3 hours until fork tender. Skim excess fat from gravy. Makes 6 servings.

Round steak is 3 cuts of meat in one. Top round is most tender and expensive. Eye of round is less. Bottom round is least expensive, ideal for Swiss steak.

Hunt's All-Time Favorites

PIZZA ON THE DOUBLE
Made extra-easy with different sauces and toppings

1000 ml	4 cups sifted all-purpose flour
30 ml	2 Tablesp. baking powder
30 ml	2 Tablesp. grated Parmesan cheese
10 ml	2 teasp. salt
10 ml	2 teasp. oregano
170 ml	⅔ cup pure vegetable oil
335 ml	1⅓ cups water
	1 (8-oz./226 g) can Hunt's Tomato Sauce with Cheese
375 ml	1½ cups shredded Cheddar cheese
250 ml	1 cup chopped onion
125 ml	½ cup chopped green pepper
	1 (8-oz./226 g) can Hunt's Tomato Sauce with Mushrooms
375 ml	1½ cups shredded Monterey Jack cheese
125 ml	½ cup sliced ripe olives

Combine flour, baking powder, Parmesan, salt and oregano in a large mixing bowl. Measure oil and water into one container; pour, all at once, into flour mixture; stir to form a ball. Divide in half; place on 15-inch (38 cm) pizza or jelly roll pans; press to fit; form edges. Spread one crust with Hunt's Sauce *with Cheese*, sprinkle with Cheddar cheese, *½ cup* (125 ml) onion and green pepper. Spread second with Hunt's Sauce *with Mushrooms*, sprinkle with Monterey Jack cheese, *remaining ½ cup* (125 ml) onion and sliced olives. Bake at 450° (235°C) 15 to 20 minutes. Makes two 15-inch (38 cm) pizzas.

Hunt's All-Time Favorites

JIFFY PORCUPINES
A delicious old favorite in almost no time at all

450 g	1 lb. ground beef
170 ml	⅔ cup quick-cooking rice
60 ml	¼ cup chopped onion
5 ml	1 teasp. salt
1 ml	¼ teasp. pepper
30 ml	2 Tablesp. pure vegetable oil
	2 (8-oz./226 g) or 1 (15-oz./425 g) can Hunt's Tomato Sauce
60 ml	¼ cup water

Mix beef, rice, onion and seasonings. Form into 1-inch (3 cm) meatballs. Brown lightly on all sides in oil in 10-inch (25 cm) skillet; drain fat. Add Hunt's Sauce and water. Mix well. Cover. Simmer about 20 minutes. Makes 4 servings.

TAMALE JOE
Popular with both family and guests   11

225 g	½	lb. link sausage, cut in ½-inch (1 cm) pieces
675 g	1½	lbs. ground beef
	1	large onion, chopped
15 ml	1	Tablesp. chili powder
10 ml	2	teasp. salt
1 ml	¼	teasp. pepper
	1	(12-oz./335 g) can whole kernel corn, drained
	2	(8-oz./226 g) or 1 (15-oz./425 g) can Hunt's Tomato Sauce
250 ml	1	cup milk
125 ml	½	cup cornmeal
	1	small can pitted ripe olives, drained
250 ml	1	cup shredded process American cheese

Brown sausages, beef and onion in large skillet. Cook and stir until beef loses redness; drain fat. Add seasonings, corn, Hunt's Sauce and milk. Simmer 10 minutes. Gradually stir cornmeal into meat mixture; add olives. Pour into 2½-quart (2.5 liter) casserole and top with cheese. Bake in 350° (175°C) oven 35 to 40 minutes. Makes 6 to 8 servings.

DUTCH MEAT LOAF
One of our most often requested

675 g	1½	lbs. lean ground beef
250 ml	1	cup fresh bread crumbs
	1	medium onion, chopped
	1	(8-oz./226 g) can Hunt's Tomtato Sauce
	1	egg
8 ml	1½	teasp. salt
1 ml	¼	teasp. pepper
180 ml	¾	cup water
30 ml	2	Tablesp. brown sugar, packed
30 ml	2	Tablesp. prepared mustard
15 ml	1	Tablesp. vinegar

In medium bowl, lightly mix beef, bread crumbs, onion, ½ *can* Hunt's Sauce, egg, salt and pepper. Shape into loaf in shallow baking pan. Combine *remaining* Hunt's Sauce with rest of ingredients; pour over loaf. Bake at 350° (175°C) 1¼ hours. Baste loaf several times. Makes 5 to 6 servings.

Hunt's
All-Time
Favorites
SOUTHERN-STYLE FISH FILLETS
A marvelous standby that's easy to do

250 ml	1 cup sliced celery
60 ml	¼ cup chopped onion
30 ml	2 Tablesp. pure vegetable oil
450 g	1 lb. fish fillets
	1 (8-oz./226 g) can Hunt's Tomato Sauce
30 ml	2 Tablesp. lemon juice
15 ml	1 Tablesp. Worcestershire
5 ml	1 teasp. salt

Sauté celery and onion in oil in 10-inch (25 cm) skillet; move to outer edge. Add fillets, sauté lightly on both sides. Add remaining ingredients; mix with vegetables and spoon around and over fillets. Cover; simmer 10 to 15 minutes until fish is done. Makes 4 servings.

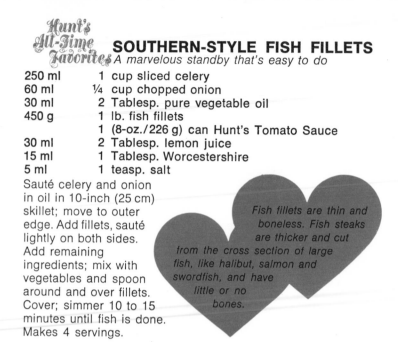

Fish fillets are thin and boneless. Fish steaks are thicker and cut from the cross section of large fish, like halibut, salmon and swordfish, and have little or no bones.

Hunt's
All-Time
Favorites
SPARERIBS ALOHA
Baked in a pineapple sweet-and-sour sauce

1400 g	3 lbs. (2 strips) lean spareribs
	Salt and pepper
125 ml	½ cup finely diced onion
60 ml	¼ cup diced green pepper
	2 (8-oz./226 g) or 1 (15-oz./425 g) can Hunt's Tomato Sauce
15 ml	1 Tablesp. Worcestershire
85 ml	⅓ cup vinegar
	2 (8-oz./226 g) cans pineapple chunks, undrained
60 ml	¼ cup brown sugar, packed
3 ml	½ teasp. dry mustard

Cut between every third rib, about halfway through the strip; sprinkle with salt and pepper. Place in shallow roasting pan. Bake at 425° (220°C) 1 hour. Carefully pour off fat. While ribs are roasting, mix remaining ingredients in medium bowl and let stand to blend flavor. Pour over ribs after 1 hour baking. Reduce temperature to 375° (190°C); bake 30 to 40 minutes longer, baste frequently. Makes 4 to 6 servings.

EASY OVEN STEW
A terrifically tasty one-dish meal

60 ml	¼ cup flour
10 ml	2 teasp. salt
1 ml	¼ teasp. pepper
1 ml	¼ teasp. paprika
900 g	2 lbs. boneless beef chuck or round, cut into 1-inch (3 cm) cubes
30 ml	2 Tablesp. pure vegetable oil
	4 small onions, quartered
	4 small carrots, pared and cut into 1-inch (3 cm) pieces
	4 small potatoes, pared and halved
250 ml	1 cup sliced celery
250 ml	1 cup water
	2 (8-oz./226 g) cans Hunt's Tomato Sauce with Mushrooms

Combine flour, salt, pepper and paprika in bag. Drop in beef, a portion at a time; shake until coated. Mix with oil in 3-quart (3 liter) casserole. Bake, uncovered, at *400°* (205°C) 30 minutes. Stir once. Add vegetables, water and Hunt's Sauce; mix well. Cover; bake at *350°* (175°C) 1¾ hours or until done. Makes 6 servings.

SPANISH RICE PRONTO
The perfect last-minute dish

	4 slices bacon, diced
125 ml	½ cup chopped onion
500 ml	2 cups quick-cooking rice
375 ml	1½ cups water
	1 (15-oz./425 g) can Hunt's Tomato Sauce with Tomato Bits
125 ml	½ cup chopped green pepper
5 ml	1 teasp. salt
5 ml	1 teasp. brown sugar, packed
3 ml	½ teasp. chili powder
250 ml	1 cup shredded Cheddar cheese

Cook bacon and onion in a 10-inch (25 cm) skillet until bacon is crisp and onion is tender; drain fat. Add remaining ingredients, *except* cheese; mix well. Bring to a boil. Cover; reduce heat and simmer 5 minutes; stir occasionally. Remove from heat; sprinkle cheese over top; cover, let stand 5 minutes before serving. Makes 4 to 6 servings.

NEW! COUNTRY PIE
Meat crust with a saucy, savory filling

	2 (8-oz./226 g) or 1 (15-oz./425 g) can Hunt's Tomato Sauce
125 ml	½ cup dry bread crumbs
450 g	1 lb. lean ground beef
60 ml	¼ cup chopped onion
60 ml	¼ cup chopped green pepper
.5 ml	⅛ teasp. pepper
.5 ml	⅛ teasp. oregano
	Salt
335 ml	1⅓ cups quick-cooking rice
250 ml	1 cup water
250 ml	1 cup shredded Cheddar cheese

Thoroughly blend ½ cup (125 ml) Hunt's Sauce with *next 6* ingredients and *1½ teaspoons* (8 ml) salt in a medium mixing bowl. Pat meat mixture evenly into bottom and around sides of a 9-inch (23 cm) deep-dish pie plate or 10-inch (25 cm) pie plate. Set aside. Combine *½ teaspoon* (3 ml) salt, rice, water, *remaining* Hunt's Sauce and *¾ cup* (180 ml) cheese. Spoon into meat shell. Cover with aluminum foil. Bake at 350° (175°C) 25 minutes. Uncover and sprinkle top with *remaining ¼ cup* (60 ml) cheese. Return to oven and bake, uncovered, 10 to 15 minutes longer. Cut into wedges to serve. Makes 5 to 6 servings.

STOVE-TOP CHICKEN BBQ
Real barbecue flavor from the top of your stove

1200 g	2½ to 3 lbs. frying chicken pieces
5 ml	1 teasp. salt
1 ml	¼ teasp. pepper
45 ml	3 Tablesp. pure vegetable oil
	1 (8-oz./226 g) can Hunt's Tomato Sauce with Onions
125 ml	½ cup water
30 ml	2 Tablesp. vinegar
15 ml	1 Tablesp. brown sugar, packed
5 ml	1 teasp. Worcestershire
3 ml	½ teasp. salt

Season chicken with salt and pepper. Brown in oil in 10-inch (25 cm) skillet; drain fat. Combine remaining ingredients; pour over chicken. Cover; simmer, basting several times, 45 minutes or until chicken is tender. Makes 4 servings.

HUNT'S 5-MINUTE ASPIC
Tastes like it took hours to make

	1 (3-oz./85 g) pkg. lemon-flavored gelatin
310 ml	1¼ cups boiling water
	1 (8-oz./226 g) can Hunt's Tomato Sauce
15 ml	1 Tablesp. vinegar
3 ml	½ teasp. seasoned salt
	Dash white pepper
	3 drops Tabasco

Dissolve gelatin in boiling water in small bowl. Add remaining ingredients; mix thoroughly. Pour into 4 individual molds or a small ring mold. Chill until firm. Unmold on salad greens. Serve ring mold filled with cottage cheese or chicken or seafood salad. Serve individual molds, as desired, with mayonnaise, sour cream or garnish of sliced hard-cooked egg, avocado crescents or sliced cucumber. Makes 4 to 6 servings.

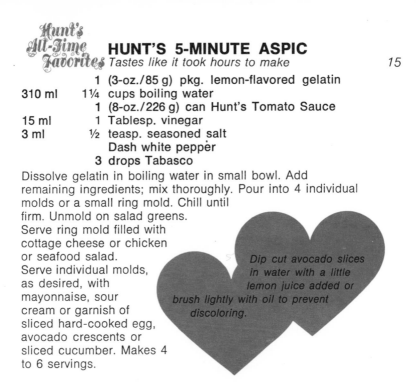

Dip cut avocado slices in water with a little lemon juice added or brush lightly with oil to prevent discoloring.

MINUTE STEAK STEW
Quick and easy dinner—perfect for a busy day

675 g	1½ lbs. cube or minute steaks
60 ml	¼ cup flour
5 ml	1 teasp. salt
1 ml	¼ teasp. pepper
1 ml	¼ teasp. paprika
30 ml	2 Tablesp. pure vegetable oil
	1 (15-oz./425 g) can Hunt's Tomato Sauce
	1 (16-oz./454 g) can mixed peas and carrots, drained (or 2 cups/500 ml cooked peas and carrots)
	8 to 10 small potatoes (cooked or canned)
30 ml	2 Tablesp. finely chopped onion

Cut steaks into 1- x 2-inch (3 x 5 cm) strips. Combine flour, salt, pepper and paprika in bag. Shake steak strips, a few at a time, in flour mixture until coated. Brown on both sides in oil in 12-inch (30 cm) skillet; drain fat. Stir in remaining ingredients. Cover; simmer 10 minutes. Makes 6 servings.

CHICKEN MARENGO

A simple company dish that's sure to please

	1 (2½- to 3-lb./1200 g) frying chicken, cut up
60 ml	¼ cup flour
5 ml	1 teasp. salt
1 ml	¼ teasp. pepper
30 ml	2 Tablesp. pure vegetable oil
	1 clove garlic, crushed
	2 (8-oz./226 g) or 1 (15-oz./425 g) can Hunt's Tomato Sauce
125 ml	½ cup chicken bouillon
	1 (4-oz./114 g) can sliced mushrooms, undrained

Lightly coat chicken with mixture of flour, salt and pepper. Brown in 12-inch (30 cm) skillet in oil until golden. Add garlic and remaining ingredients. Cover; simmer about 45 to 50 minutes until chicken is tender. Makes 4 to 5 servings.

CABBAGE ROLLS

A sweet-tart European favorite that's quick and easy to do

	1 large head cabbage
675 g	1½ lbs. ground beef and pork for meat loaf
	1 small onion, minced
10 ml	2 teasp. salt
3 ml	½ teasp. pepper
180 ml	¾ cup cooked rice
	2 (8-oz./226 g) cans Hunt's Tomato Sauce
60 ml	¼ cup brown sugar, packed
60 ml	¼ cup lemon juice or vinegar

Core cabbage and place cored side up in deep bowl or saucepan. *Cover* with boiling water; let stand 4 to 5 minutes to soften and loosen leaves; drain. Remove 12 large leaves and reserve. Cook meat and onion in 10-inch (25 cm) skillet until onion is tender; drain fat. Add salt, pepper, rice and *1 can* Hunt's Sauce. Place portions of meat mixture in center of each cabbage leaf. Roll up, folding ends over. Place seam side down in 7½- x 12- x 1½-inch (18 x 30 x 4 cm) baking dish. Mix *remaining can* Hunt's Sauce, brown sugar and lemon juice. Pour over rolls. Cover, bake at 375° (190°C) 30 minutes. Uncover, baste cabbage rolls, bake 15 minutes longer. Makes 6 servings.

7-LAYER CASSEROLE

No pre-cooking needed for this colorful, one-dish meal

250 ml	1 cup uncooked rice
	1 (1-lb./450 g) can whole kernel corn, undrained
5 ml	1 teasp. seasoned salt
1 ml	¼ teasp. seasoned pepper
	1 beef bouillon cube
180 ml	·¾ cup boiling water
	1 (15-oz./425 g) can Hunt's Tomato Sauce with Tomato Bits
5 ml	1 teasp. Worcestershire
5 ml	1 teasp. Italian herb seasoning
250 ml	1 cup chopped onion
125 ml	½ cup *each:* chopped green pepper and celery
450 g	1 lb. lean ground beef
250 ml	1 cup shredded mild Cheddar cheese
30 ml	2 Tablesp. imitation bacon bits

In 2-quart (2 liter) casserole, arrange ingredients in layers in the following order:

1. Rice mixed well with corn, *half* the salt and pepper, bouillon cube and boiling water.
2. Half of Hunt's Sauce that has been mixed with Worcestershire and Italian seasoning.

Italian herb seasoning is a bottled blend of marjoram, thyme, rosemary, savory, sage, oregano and sweet basil handy for spicing up any dish.

3. Chopped onion, green pepper and celery.
4. Uncooked ground beef, *remaining* salt and pepper.
5. *Remaining* Hunt's Sauce mixture. Cover tightly; bake at 375° (190°C) 45 minutes.
6. Sprinkle with cheese; bake, *uncovered,* 15 minutes longer.
7. Top with bacon bits before serving. Makes 4 to 6 servings.

Around the U.S.A. in 14 Recipes

In this chapter we've included some real American recipes to take you on a cooking tour of the country. There are New England dishes that date back to the days of the Pilgrims, and delicate Creole dishes from the deep, deep South. And after we sample some hearty midwestern fare, we travel on to taste the Indian-influenced dishes of the Southwest, on up the coast to the special food of the Pacific Northwest.

You'll love all this authentic American cuisine, no matter what part of the country you're from.

Opposite: Hand-Me-Down Meat Loaf

HAND-ME-DOWN MEAT LOAF

A midwestern recipe every generation treasures

675 g	1½	lbs. lean ground beef
250 ml	1	cup fine cracker crumbs
125 ml	½	cup chopped onion
125 ml	½	cup chopped green pepper
	1	egg
	1	(15-oz./425 g) can Hunt's Tomato Sauce with Tomato Bits
3 ml	½	teasp. salt
1 ml	¼	teasp. pepper
60 ml	¼	cup water
15 ml	1	Tablesp. brown sugar, packed

Mix together in bowl, ground beef, cracker crumbs, onion, green pepper and egg with ½ *can* Hunt's Sauce, salt and pepper. Shape into loaf in shallow baking pan. Bake at 350° (175°C) 1 hour. Drain fat. Add water and brown sugar to *remaining* Hunt's Sauce; pour over loaf; bake 20 minutes longer. Spoon pan sauce over top before serving. Makes 6 servings.

BOSTON BAKED BEANS[C]

An old-fashioned favorite cooked the old-fashioned way

450 g	1	lb. navy beans
		Water
15 ml	1	Tablesp. vinegar
5 ml	1	teasp. salt
	1	(8-oz./226 g) can Hunt's Tomato Sauce
85 ml	⅓	cup brown sugar, packed
85 ml	⅓	cup molasses
55 g	¼	lb. salt pork, cut into 4 pieces
	1	small onion, quartered
15 ml	1	Tablesp. prepared mustard

Cover beans with water. Bring to a boil for 2 minutes. Remove from heat, cover; let stand 1 hour. Add vinegar, salt and additional water to cover the beans. Bring to boil again; simmer, covered, 1½ hours until bean skins crack. Pour into bean pot or casserole. Stir in remaining ingredients and additional water just to cover. Bake, covered, at 275° (135°C) about 5 hours. Add a little water during baking if beans start to dry out. Makes 6 servings.

C *Slow Cooker*

Opposite: Boston Baked Beans

MANHATTAN CLAM CHOWDER
So delicious, it's popular even in Boston

	3 slices bacon, cut into ½-inch (1 cm) pieces
125 ml	½ cup chopped onion
125 ml	½ cup diced celery
375 ml	1½ cups water
250 ml	1 cup diced potatoes
	1 carrot, shredded
5 ml	1 teasp. salt
	1 (8-oz./226 g) can Hunt's Tomato Sauce
	1 (8-oz./226 g) can minced clams, undrained
1 ml	¼ teasp. leaf thyme

In 3-quart (3 liter) saucepan, brown bacon until crisp. Add onion and celery, sauté until onion is soft. Drain fat. Add water, potatoes, carrots and salt. Cover, simmer 20 minutes. Add Hunt's Sauce, clams and thyme. Heat through. Makes 4 (1-cup/250 ml) servings.

POOR MAN'S CIOPPINO
A sensational seafood stew from San Francisco

250 ml	1 cup chopped onion
125 ml	½ cup chopped green pepper
125 ml	½ cup chopped carrot
125 ml	½ cup chopped celery
	1 clove garlic, minced
30 ml	2 Tablesp. pure vegetable oil
	1 (15-oz./425 g) can Hunt's Tomato Sauce
625 ml	2½ cups water
125 ml	½ cup dry red wine
	1 vegetable bouillon cube
3 ml	½ teasp. Italian herb seasoning
3 ml	½ teasp. salt
.5 ml	⅛ teasp. seasoned pepper
225 g	½ lb. halibut cut into 1-inch (3 cm) pieces
170 g	6 ozs. cooked shrimp
	1 (6-oz./170 g) pkg. frozen snow crab, thawed
	Minced parsley

In Dutch oven, sauté onion, green pepper, carrot, celery and garlic in oil until onion is soft. Stir in Hunt's Sauce, water, wine, bouillon cube, Italian seasoning, salt and pepper. Cover; simmer 15 minutes. Stir occasionally. Add halibut, shrimp and crab. Cover; simmer 20 minutes longer. Sprinkle servings with minced parsley. Makes 8 (1-cup/250 ml) servings.

CORN PUDDING

A corn belt favorite with a whole new flavor   23

125 ml	½ cup *each:* minced onion and green pepper
15 ml	1 Tablesp. butter
500 ml	2 cups frozen whole kernel corn, cooked and drained
15 ml	1 Tablesp. flour
250 ml	1 cup whipping cream
	1 (8-oz./226 g) can Hunt's Tomato Sauce
	3 eggs, beaten
10 ml	2 to 3 teasp. curry powder
5 ml	1 teasp. salt
3 ml	½ teasp. sugar

In a small skillet, sauté onion and green pepper in butter until tender. Add corn and flour; toss to mix. Combine whipping cream, Hunt's Sauce, eggs, curry powder, salt and sugar in a well-buttered 1½-quart (1.5 liter) casserole or soufflé dish; blend well. Stir in corn mixture. Bake at 350° (175°C) 1 to 1¼ hours or until knife inserted in center comes out clean. Makes 8 servings.

BARBECUED BEEF BURGERS

Saucy and spicy from the real Midwest

	1 (8-oz./226 g) can Hunt's Tomato Sauce
125 ml	½ cup ketchup
125 ml	½ cup bottled barbecue sauce
60 ml	¼ cup vinegar
	2 lemons
30 ml	2 Tablesp. sugar
15 ml	1 Tablesp. minced onion
5 ml	1 teasp. garlic salt
	Few drops Tabasco
	Dash cayenne
900 g	2 lbs. lean ground beef
	8 hamburger buns, toasted

This is an all-purpose barbecue-basting sauce equally good on chicken, pork, ribs and steaks.

In medium saucepan, combine Hunt's Sauce, ketchup, barbecue sauce and vinegar; mix well. Stir in the *juice* from lemons, sugar, onion, garlic salt and add Tabasco and cayenne to taste. Simmer together 10 minutes; stir occasionally. Cool slightly. Add *1 cup* (250 ml) of above sauce to ground beef in bowl and mix thoroughly. Form into 8 patties. Grill or broil to desired doneness, brushing frequently with *remaining* sauce. Serve between toasted buns. Makes 8 beef burgers.

AROUND THE U.S.A. IN 14 RECIPES

SHEEPHERDER'S STEW[C]

A handsome, hearty stew from the mountains of Montana

900 g	2 lbs. boneless lamb, cut into 2-inch (5 cm) pieces
60 ml	¼ cup flour
8 ml	1½ teasp. seasoned salt
5 ml	1 teasp. garlic powder
1 ml	¼ teasp. pepper
45 ml	3 Tablesp. pure vegetable oil
	2 (15-oz./425 g) cans Hunt's Tomato Sauce with Tomato Bits
	1 beef bouillon cube
	1 bay leaf
	4 medium potatoes, quartered
	4 carrots, quartered
	2 small onions, quartered
	1 (10-oz./283 g) pkg. frozen cut green beans

Coat lamb with mixture of flour, *1 teaspoon* (5 ml) salt, garlic powder and pepper. Brown in oil in 12-inch (30 cm) skillet. Drain fat. Add Hunt's Sauce, bouillon cube, bay leaf and *remaining* salt. Cover, simmer 1 hour. Add vegetables; simmer 30 minutes. Makes 6 to 8 servings.

[C]*Slow Cooker*

AROUND THE U.S.A. IN 14 RECIPES

SALMON BURGERS

Seattle's answer to Grandmother's croquettes

	1 (16-oz./450 g) can red or pink salmon
60 ml	¼ cup minced onion
125 ml	½ cup fine dry bread crumbs
125 ml	½ cup chopped parsley
	1 (8-oz./226 g) can Hunt's Tomato Sauce with Cheese
	1 egg
5 ml	1 teasp. dry mustard
3 ml	½ teasp. salt
	Pure vegetable oil
	6 hamburger buns

Drain and flake salmon into small bowl. Add remaining ingredients, *except* oil and buns. Mix well. Divide into six equal portions; shape into patties. Roll each in *additional* bread crumbs. Fry in ½ inch (1 cm) of oil about 3 minutes on each side or until golden brown. Drain on paper towel. Serve on buns with desired condiments. Makes 6 servings.

LOUISIANA EGGS CREOLE

Serve with sour cream for brunch or supper   25

225 g	½ lb. pork sausage links, cut into 1-inch (3 cm) pieces
125 ml	½ cup finely chopped green pepper
60 ml	¼ cup finely chopped onion
	1 (15-oz./425 g) can Hunt's Tomato Sauce Special
	8 eggs
85 ml	⅓ cup milk
5 ml	1 teasp. fines herbes
3 ml	½ teasp. salt
	Butter
	4 to 6 slices hot buttered toast

Brown sausage links in shallow saucepan. Add green pepper and onion and cook until onion is soft. Drain fat. Add Hunt's Sauce. Simmer 5 minutes. Keep warm. In medium bowl, combine eggs, milk, fines herbes and salt. Blend well. In 10-inch (25 cm) skillet, scramble eggs in butter over medium heat. Place equal portions of eggs on each slice of toast. Spoon equal portions of creole sauce over eggs. Makes 4 to 6 servings.

SAUERKRAUT AND KNACKWURST

Here's one that really made Milwaukee famous

	1 (2-lb./900 g) can sauerkraut
	1 (12-oz./340 g) pkg. knackwurst, cut into 1-inch (3 cm) pieces
	3 slices bacon, cut into 1-inch (3 cm) pieces
	1 large onion, thinly sliced
	1 (15-oz./425 g) can Hunt's Tomato Sauce Special
875 ml	3½ cups water
	2 tart apples, peeled, cored and sliced
	6 peppercorns
10 ml	2 teasp. seasoned salt
10 ml	2 teasp. caraway seed
500 ml	2 cups hot prepared mashed potatoes
1 ml	¼ teasp. white pepper

In a medium bowl, rinse and soak sauerkraut in cold water for 10 minutes; drain. Sauté knackwurst, bacon and onion in a large kettle or Dutch oven until bacon is slightly crisp. Stir in Hunt's Sauce, water, sauerkraut, apple slices, peppercorns, *1 teasp. (5 ml) each:* seasoned salt and caraway seed. Simmer 50 to 55 minutes, stirring occasionally. Combine *remaining 1 teasp. (5 ml) each:* seasoned salt and caraway seed with potatoes and pepper. Drop by tablespoonfuls onto sauerkraut mixture; simmer 5 minutes longer. Makes 6 to 8 servings.

AROUND THE U.S.A. IN 14 RECIPES · REAL TEXAS CHILI

A secret ingredient makes it extra thick and extra rich

225 g	½ lb. chorizo
225 g	½ lb. ground beef
375 ml	1½ cups chopped onion
	2 cloves garlic, minced
	1 (15-oz./425 g) can Hunt's Tomato Sauce with Tomato Bits
	1 (15½-oz./439 g) can small red beans, undrained
	1 (8-oz./226 g) can refried beans
45 ml	3 to 4 Tablesp. chili powder
5 ml	1 teasp. ground cumin
5 ml	1 teasp. oregano
3 ml	½ teasp. salt

In 3-quart (3 liter) saucepan, cook chorizo, beef, *1 cup* (250 ml) onion and garlic until onion is soft; spoon off excess fat. Add Hunt's Sauce, red beans, refried beans and seasonings; mix thoroughly. Cover, simmer 20 minutes; stir once or twice. To serve, spoon chili into individual serving bowls and top with equal amounts of *remaining* chopped onion. Makes 5 (1-cup/250 ml) servings.

AROUND THE U.S.A. IN 14 RECIPES · JAMBALAYA

CREOLE HAM AND RICE
A southern tradition with world-famous flavor

375 g	1½ cups diced cooked ham
250 ml	1 cup chopped onion
180 ml	¾ cup sliced celery
	1 medium green pepper, cut into thin strips
	1 clove garlic, minced
30 ml	2 Tablesp. pure vegetable oil
	1 (10¾-oz./305 g) can chicken broth
	1 (15-oz./425 g) can Hunt's Tomato Sauce
250 ml	1 cup chopped cooked chicken
180 ml	¾ cup uncooked rice
30 ml	2 Tablesp. minced parsley
	1 bay leaf
1 ml	¼ teasp. leaf thyme
1 ml	¼ teasp. Worcestershire
.5 ml	⅛ teasp. cayenne

Cook ham, onion, celery, green pepper and garlic in oil in large skillet until onion is soft. Add remaining ingredients. Bring to a boil. Cover; simmer 30 minutes, stirring once or twice. Makes 4 to 6 servings.

FAMILY-RECIPE GOULASH

Quick and easy from down Missouri way   27

250 ml	1 cup small shell macaroni
	Boiling water
450 g	1 lb. ground beef
	1 medium onion, chopped
500 ml	2 cups sliced celery
	1 (2-oz./56 g) can sliced mushrooms, undrained
	1 (15-oz./425 g) can Hunt's Tomato Sauce with Tomato Bits
125 ml	½ cup ketchup
5 ml	1 teasp. salt
1 ml	¼ teasp. pepper

Place macaroni in small bowl; cover with boiling water; set aside. While macaroni blanches, cook ground beef and onion together in a large skillet about 7 to 8 minutes, until meat is brown and onion tender. Drain fat. Drain macaroni thoroughly and add to skillet along with celery, mushrooms, Hunt's Sauce, ketchup, seasonings and *1 cup* (250 ml) water. Mix thoroughly. Cover; simmer 30 minutes, stirring occasionally. Makes 6 (1-cup/250 ml) servings.

SOUTHWESTERN SUPPER

Classic casserole in every region of the country

450 g	1 lb. ground beef
	1 onion, chopped
	1 clove garlic, minced
	1 (15-oz./425 g) can Hunt's Tomato Sauce with Tomato Bits
	1 (1-lb./454 g) can whole kernel corn, drained
10 ml	2 teasp. salt
10 ml	2 to 3 teasp. chili powder
	1 (2½-oz./70 g) can sliced ripe olives
180 ml	¾ cup cornmeal
250 ml	1 cup milk
	2 eggs, well beaten
375 ml	1½ cups shredded sharp Cheddar cheese

Brown beef in skillet; add onion and garlic and cook until onion is soft. Drain fat. Add Hunt's Sauce, corn, *1 teaspoon* (5 ml) salt and chili powder. Cover; simmer 15 minutes. Pour into 7½- x 12- x 1½-inch (18 x 30 x 4 cm) baking pan. Top with sliced olives. In small bowl, combine cornmeal, milk, eggs and *remaining* salt; pour over filling. Sprinkle with cheese. Bake at 350° (175°C) 40 to 45 minutes. Makes 6 to 8 servings.

Entertaining on a Budget

Entertaining at home doesn't have
to be an expensive affair, not when
you follow the recipes in this chapter.
Whether you're planning a lavish sit-down
dinner for ten or a simple brunch, you'll find
just the recipe you're looking for.

And for especially relaxed
hostessing, we've included some recipes
you can prepare ahead. They're all
delicious, and all
delightful—budget-wise.

Opposite: Sassy Beef Crêpes (page 33)

EGGPLANT NAPOLI^M

Cheese makes the meal . . . for less

	1	(15-oz./425 g) can Hunt's Tomato Sauce Special
125 ml	½	cup water
125 ml	½	cup chopped onion
	1	(1½-oz./45 g) env. spaghetti sauce mix
5 ml	1	teasp. seasoned salt
	1	large eggplant, pared and sliced
225 g	8	ozs. mozzarella cheese, thinly sliced
60 ml	¼	cup grated Parmesan cheese

Combine *first five* ingredients in saucepan; blend well. Heat to boiling; simmer 5 minutes. Arrange alternate layers of sauce mixture, eggplant and cheese slices in a 7½- x 12- x 1½-inch (18 x 30 x 4 cm) baking dish, starting and ending with sauce mixture. Top with Parmesan cheese. Bake at 375° (190°C) 30 to 40 minutes. Makes 6 servings.

^M*Microwave*

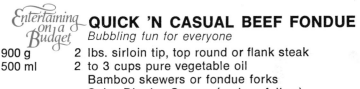

Entertaining on a Budget

QUICK 'N CASUAL BEEF FONDUE

Bubbling fun for everyone

900 g	2 lbs. sirloin tip, top round or flank steak
500 ml	2 to 3 cups pure vegetable oil
	Bamboo skewers or fondue forks
	Spicy Dipping Sauces (recipes follow)

Trim all fat from meat; cut into thin bite-size cubes. Pile in serving bowl; refrigerate until ready to cook. Heat oil in 1½-quart (1.5 liter) heavy saucepan to 375°* (190°C). Transfer to metal fondue pot for serving, keeping hot over canned heat. Allow guests to spear cubes of meat on skewers or fondue forks; immerse in hot oil from 30 seconds to a minute, cooking to desired doneness. Dip in choice of Spicy Dipping Sauces. Makes 4 to 6 servings.

Spicy Dipping Sauces: Combine in 1-quart (1 liter) saucepan 2 (8-oz./226 g) cans Hunt's Tomato Sauce with Mushrooms, 1 tablespoon (15 ml) *each:* grated onion, lemon juice and chopped parsley, 1 clove garlic, crushed, and 2 tablespoons (30 ml) bacon bits. Simmer, uncovered, 20 minutes. To *half* of this basic sauce, stir in ¼ cup (60 ml) sour cream and 1 teaspoon (5 ml) *each:* chives and dill seed.

*Always use a deep-fat frying thermometer for accurate temperature control and safety. Never add oil for deep frying to more than ⅓ the depth of the pan or fondue pot.

Opposite: Quick 'n Casual Beef Fondue

Entertaining on a Budget

POLYNESIAN SHORT RIBS
An exotic, tropical dish

1600 g	3½ to 4 lbs. beef short ribs
13 ml	2½ teasp. meat tenderizer
	1 (15-oz./425 g) can Hunt's Tomato Sauce
125 ml	½ cup soy sauce
60 ml	¼ cup pure vegetable oil
60 ml	¼ cup chopped onion
60 ml	¼ cup sugar
30 ml	2 Tablesp. toasted sesame seed
5 ml	1 teasp. monosodium glutamate
3 ml	½ teasp. garlic powder
1 ml	¼ teasp. *each:* salt and pepper

Remove meat from ribs; cut into 1-inch (3 cm) cubes; sprinkle with meat tenderizer; toss to coat. Place in a 7½- x 12- x 1½-inch (18 x 30 x 4 cm) glass baking dish. Combine remaining ingredients in small bowl; mix well. Pour over meat cubes. Marinate, covered, in refrigerator overnight. Drain meat, *reserving* marinade. Broil on rack or grill about 2 inches (5 cm) from source of heat 10 to 15 minutes or until brown. Turn often. Heat reserved marinade in small saucepan to boiling point; lower heat and simmer a minute or two. Use as a dip for meat cubes or a sauce for rice or noodles. Makes 6 to 8 servings.

Entertaining on a Budget

CHEESE LASAGNA^M
Your guests won't miss the meat at all

	1 (15-oz./425 g) can Hunt's Tomato Sauce with Tomato Bits
	½ cup minced onion
125 ml	½ to 1 teasp. garlic powder
5 ml	2 teasp. seasoned salt
10 ml	2 teasp. Italian herb seasoning
10 ml	2 eggs, beaten
	1 (16-oz./454 g) carton ricotta or cottage cheese
	1 (8-oz./225 g) pkg. lasagna noodles, cooked
450 g	1 lb. mozzarella cheese, thinly sliced
60 ml	¼ cup grated Parmesan cheese

Combine Hunt's Sauce, onion, garlic powder, seasoned salt and Italian seasoning. Blend eggs with ricotta. Spoon a little sauce mixture into a 9- x 13- x 1½-inch (23 x 33 x 4 cm) baking dish to coat bottom; arrange a layer of *half* each: noodles, ricotta mixture, sauce mixture and mozzarella. Repeat. Sprinkle with Parmesan. Bake at 350° (175°C) 45 minutes. Let stand 10 minutes before cutting. Makes 6 servings.

^M*Microwave*

STUFFED PORK LOIN
A simple supper that's easy to carve

1600 g	3½ to 4 lb. boneless pork loin
	Salt and pepper
750 ml	3 cups melba toast stuffing mix
60 ml	¼ cup grated Parmesan cheese
30 ml	2 Tablesp. chopped parsley
15 ml	1 Tablesp. Worcestershire
3 ml	½ teasp. garlic powder
	1 (8-oz./226 g) can Hunt's Tomato Sauce

Using a sharp knife, cut a deep pocket lengthwise in pork loin. Sprinkle with salt and pepper. Combine remaining ingredients in bowl; mix well. Use to fill pork loin pocket. Secure with toothpicks or kitchen string. Bake at 375° (190°C) about 1½ hours. Makes 10 to 12 servings.

SASSY BEEF CREPES
A gourmet dish for Sunday brunch

225 g	½ lb. ground beef
125 ml	½ cup *each:* chopped onion and green pepper
	1 (15-oz./425 g) can Hunt's Tomato Sauce with Tomato Bits
8 ml	¾ teasp. salt
3 ml	½ teasp. *each:* oregano and chili powder
1 ml	¼ teasp. garlic powder (optional)
.5 ml	⅛ teasp. pepper
	8 Crêpes (recipe follows)
60 ml	¼ cup shredded Cheddar cheese

In 10-inch (25 cm) frying pan, sauté beef, onion and green pepper until beef loses redness. Drain fat. Add ½ *can* Hunt's Sauce and seasonings. Fill crêpes one at a time in 1-quart (1 liter) shallow baking dish, spooning equal amount of meat mixture down center of each and folding sides to overlap. Pour *remaining* Hunt's Sauce down center; top with cheese. Bake at 425° (220°C) 5 to 10 minutes. Makes 4 servings.

Crêpes: In blender container, combine ⅓ cup (85 ml) *each:* milk and water, 1 whole egg and 1 egg yolk. Add ½ cup (125 ml) sifted all-purpose flour, ⅛ teaspoon (.5 ml) salt and 1 tablespoon (15 ml) melted butter; blend. Heat 8-inch (20 cm) crêpe pan over high heat. Remove pan from heat; brush lightly with melted butter. Pour in a scant 3 tablespoons (45 ml) batter, tilting pan to thinly coat bottom. Return to heat. When crêpe is lightly browned, turn and brown other side. Makes 8 crêpes. (See photo, page 29)

Entertaining on a Budget SPICY BARBECUED SPARERIBS
A western favorite everywhere

	2	strips (about 5½ to 6 lbs./2500 g each) pork spareribs, cracked
375 ml	1½	cups minced onion
	2	large cloves garlic, minced
30 ml	2	Tablesp. pure vegetable oil
	1	(8-oz./226 g) can Hunt's Tomato Sauce
125 ml	½	cup *each:* ketchup and wine vinegar
85 ml	⅓	cup lemon juice
60 ml	¼	cup Worcestershire
60 ml	¼	cup brown sugar, packed
20 ml	4	teasp. chili powder
10 ml	2	teasp. ground celery seed
5 ml	1	teasp. ground cumin

Place spareribs on hot grill approximately 5 inches (13 cm) from coals or source of heat. Cook 45 minutes to 1 hour, turning frequently. Meanwhile, in a small pan, sauté onion and garlic in oil until onion is transparent. Add remaining ingredients. Heat to boiling. Reduce heat; simmer, uncovered, 25 to 30 minutes. Use to baste spareribs last 10 to 15 minutes of grilling; turn and baste often. Makes 10 to 12 servings.

Entertaining on a Budget STIR-FRY BEEF
When you stir fry, the trick is to be quick

	1	(8-oz./226 g) can Hunt's Tomato Sauce
60 ml	¼	cup soy sauce
20 ml	4	teasp. cornstarch
1 ml	¼	teasp. garlic powder
.5 ml	⅛	teasp. pepper
675 g	1½	lbs. top sirloin steak, trimmed
45 ml	3	Tablesp. pure vegetable oil
	1	large green pepper, sliced
375 ml	1½	cups diagonally sliced celery
	1	(4-oz./114 g) can sliced mushrooms, drained
30 ml	2	Tablesp. chopped pimiento
750 ml	3	cups hot cooked rice

Combine Hunt's Sauce, soy sauce, cornstarch, garlic powder and pepper; set aside. Slice steak into thin strips. Sauté in large skillet or wok in oil over high heat until beef loses its redness; stir constantly. Add vegetables and pimiento. Continue to stir and cook over high heat until vegetables are crisp-tender. Add Hunt's Sauce mixture to meat and vegetables; mix well. Cook 5 to 7 minutes longer or until sauce is thickened and transparent. Serve over rice. Makes 4 to 6 servings.

CHILI FOR-THE-CROWD^C
A super success every time

900 g	2 lbs. coarse ground beef or chili meat
15 ml	1 Tablesp. chili powder
10 ml	2 teasp. salt
5 ml	1 teasp. sugar
375 ml	1½ cups chopped onion
125 ml	½ cup minced green pepper
	2 (15-oz./425 g) or 1 (29-oz./822 g) can Hunt's Tomato Sauce
250 ml	1 cup water
	1 clove garlic, crushed
	1 pinch ground cumin (optional)
	1 (1-lb. 14-oz./850 g) can small red beans, undrained

Cook meat in Dutch oven or heavy kettle until it loses redness. Sprinkle with chili powder, salt and sugar; blend well through meat. Add onion and green pepper; cook, stirring occasionally, until vegetables soften. Add Hunt's Sauce, water, garlic and cumin; simmer, covered, 1 to 1½ hours. Add beans; simmer, uncovered. ½ hour or until desired consistency. Makes 2½ quarts (2.5 liters).

Make this a "kitchen party." Serve tortilla chips, a colorful relish platter and bowls of Parmesan cheese and sour cream for chili garni.

NOTE: This chili may be served at once with pride for excellent appearance and flavor. Or, it may be handled in the following suggested ways:

1. Use 1 quart (1 liter) for 1-cup (250 ml) servings for 4 people for at-once serving. Pour remainder into 1½-quart (1.5 liter) oblong baking dish; cover with foil; refrigerate 2 to 3 days to mellow seasonings. Reheat in oven at 325° (165°C) 45 minutes to 1 hour. Makes second meal of 4 to 6 servings.
2. Line 3-quart (3 liter) oblong baking dish with foil, allowing enough to bring up over top for a double fold. Pour chili in; secure foil over top and at sides; freeze. When frozen, remove foil covered block from baking dish; store frozen until ready to use. To serve: remove foil from chili-block, place in 3-quart (3 liters) oblong baking dish, cover lightly; heat in 300° (150°C) oven for 1½ to 2 hours. Stir occasionally after first hour.

^C*Slow Cooker*

MANICOTTI AS YOU LIKE IT

Put a smile on your budget with this 1-hour dish

8 manicotti shells
Cheese or Spinach Filling
1 (15-oz./425 g) can Hunt's Tomato Herb Sauce
125 ml ½ cup *each:* water and burgundy wine

Cheese Filling

225 g	8 ozs. ricotta or cottage cheese
225 g	8 ozs. mozzarella cheese, diced
60 ml	¼ cup grated Parmesan cheese
15 ml	1 Tablesp. chopped parsley
5 ml	1 teasp. seasoned salt
1 ml	¼ teasp. white pepper
1 ml	¼ teasp. garlic powder

Spinach Filling

	1 (10-oz./283 g) pkg. frozen chopped spinach, thawed and pressed very dry
225 g	8 ozs. ricotta or cottage cheese
60 ml	¼ cup grated Parmesan cheese
	2 eggs, slightly beaten
4 ml	¾ teasp. salt
.5 ml	⅛ teasp. nutmeg

Place manicotti shells in 7½- x 12- x 1½-inch (18 x 30 x 4 cm) baking dish, cover with boiling water; let stand about 5 minutes; rinse in cold water, drain thoroughly. Combine, in small bowl, ingredients for *either* Cheese or Spinach Filling; mix well. Fill drained manicotti shells with mixture. Return filled shells to baking dish. Combine Hunt's Sauce, water and wine; blend well. Pour over filled manicotti shells. Bake, covered, at 375° (190°C) 45 minutes or until *al dente*. Serve with additional Parmesan, if desired. Makes 4 servings.

Blanching manicotti shells makes them easier to handle. Use the same method for other pasta. The dish will cook faster and be less starchy.

FROMAGE-STUFFED MEAT ROLL
Easy to make. Elegant to serve 37

675 g	1½ lbs. extra lean ground beef
125 ml	½ cup fine dry bread crumbs
	1 egg
3 ml	½ teasp. garlic powder
5 ml	1 teasp. salt
	1 (8-oz./226 g) can Hunt's Tomato Sauce with Onions
56 g	2 to 4 ozs. blue cheese

Combine beef, bread crumbs, egg, garlic, salt, and ½ *can* Hunt's Sauce in medium bowl; mix well. On waxed paper, shape meat mixture in rectangle, ½ inch (1 cm) thick. Crumble blue cheese over surface. Starting with short end, roll up jelly-roll fashion. Place in shallow baking dish. Bake at 350° (175°C) 35 to 40 minutes. Pour *remaining* Hunt's Sauce over meat roll last 5 minutes of baking. Makes 6 to 8 servings.

SPAGHETTI DINNER FOR FIFTY
MARINARA SAUCE
You'll need big pots for this one

1800 g	4 lbs. lean ground beef
	4 large onions, chopped
	4 large cloves garlic, minced
	14 (15-oz./425 g) or 7 (29-oz./822 g) cans Hunt's Tomato Sauce
1500 ml	1½ quarts water
60 ml	¼ cup brown sugar, packed
30 ml	2 Tablesp. salt
10 ml	2 teasp. basil
10 ml	2 teasp. oregano
3 kg 150 g	7 lbs. spaghetti, cooked and drained

In large kettle, sauté ground beef, onion and garlic until beef loses redness and onions are transparent; drain excess fat. Stir in remaining ingredients, *except* spaghetti. Simmer, uncovered, 1 hour, stirring occasionally. Serve over hot cooked spaghetti. Makes 50 (½-cup/125 ml) servings.

MENU:
Spaghetti with Marinara
  Sauce
Tossed Green Salad with
  Tangy Italian Dressing
Garlic Bread
Spumoni Ice Cream
Coffee, Tea, Milk

SHORTCUT PIZZAS

Makes entertaining easy on the cook

	2 (1-lb./450 g) loaves frozen enriched bread dough
	1 (15-oz./425 g) can Hunt's Tomato Sauce
60 ml	¼ cup grated Parmesan cheese
10 ml	2 teasp. Italian herb seasoning
5 ml	1 teasp. seasoned salt
3 ml	½ teasp. garlic powder
3 ml	½ teasp. sugar
750 ml	3 cups shredded mozzarella cheese

Suggested Toppings

Crumbled Italian sausage
Thinly sliced Italian dry salami and pepperoni
Strips of bell pepper
Thinly sliced onion rings
Sliced mushrooms
Sliced ripe olives
Diced canned green chilies
Anchovies

Thaw loaves of bread dough according to package directions. Roll out each loaf on a lightly floured surface to fit a 15-inch (38 cm) pizza or jelly roll pan. Combine Hunt's Sauce, Parmesan cheese, Italian seasoning, salt, garlic powder and sugar; mix well. Use *half* the sauce mixture to coat the entire surface of each pizza. Sprinkle each with *1½ cups* (375 ml) cheese. Top with any or all of suggested toppings. Bake at 450° (230°C) 12 to 15 minutes. Makes two 15-inch (38 cm) pizzas.

*Be an at-ease hostess.
Make up a dish like pizza
on foil-lined pan.
Remove from pan; seal
in foil to freeze.
Bake as desired.*

HANDSOME SOLE AU GRATIN^M

As delicious as it is nutritious

675 g	1½ lbs. fillet of sole or white fish
30 ml	2 Tablesp. lemon juice
125 ml	½ cup chopped onion
30 ml	2 Tablesp. butter
	1 (15-oz./425 g) can Hunt's Tomato Sauce with Tomato Bits
60 ml	¼ cup chopped parsley
3 ml	½ teasp. *each:* salt, pepper and sugar
	2 (10-oz./283 g) pkgs. frozen cut green beans, cooked and drained
	1 egg yolk
500 ml	2 cups prepared mashed potatoes
30 ml	2 Tablesp. grated Parmesan cheese

Cut fillets into six serving-size pieces; sprinkle with lemon juice. Roll up; secure with toothpicks and stand on end in center of 7½- x 12- x 1½-inch (18 x 30 x 4 cm) baking dish. Sauté onion in butter in small saucepan. Add Hunt's Sauce, parsley, salt, pepper and sugar; simmer 3 to 5 minutes. Pour over fillets. Spoon green beans around fillets. Blend egg yolk with potatoes; spoon in border around edge of dish. Bake at 375° (190°C) 20 minutes or until fish flakes with fork. Sprinkle with Parmesan. Bake 3 to 5 minutes longer. Makes 6 servings.

^M*Microwave*

ZUCCHINI PARMESAN^M

A grand and glorious vegetable dish

	6 medium zucchini, diagonally sliced
250 ml	1 cup diagonally sliced celery
	1 onion, thinly sliced
30 ml	2 Tablesp. pure vegetable oil
	2 (8-oz./226 g) cans Hunt's Tomato Sauce with Cheese
10 ml	2 teasp. bouquet garni
5 ml	1 teasp. seasoned salt
1 ml	¼ teasp. seasoned pepper or coarse ground pepper
60 ml	¼ cup grated Parmesan cheese

Sauté zucchini, celery and onion in oil in 10-inch (25 cm) skillet until onion is transparent. Combine remaining ingredients, *except* Parmesan. Pour over zucchini mixture; stir to mix. Cover; simmer 10 to 15 minutes, stirring occasionally. Sprinkle with Parmesan cheese before serving. Makes 6 to 8 servings.

^M*Microwave*

HUNT'S ELEGANT CHEESE SOUFFLE

Entertaining on a Budget

Serve with a salad for a super supper

45 ml	3	Tablesp. butter
75 ml	5	Tablesp. flour
1 ml	¼	teasp. *each:* salt, pepper and dry mustard
.5 ml	⅛	teasp. cayenne
	1	(15-oz./425 g) can Hunt's Tomato Sauce with Tomato Bits
180 ml	¾	cup evaporated milk
500 ml	2	cups shredded sharp Cheddar cheese
	5	eggs, separated
	1	(2½-oz./64 g) can sliced mushrooms, drained
1 ml	¼	teasp. cream of tartar

Melt butter in saucepan over low heat; blend in flour, salt, pepper, mustard and cayenne. Drain Hunt's Sauce, *reserving* tomato bits. Add drained sauce to butter mixture, stirring constantly; gradually stir in milk. Heat to just below boiling. Add cheese, stirring until melted; set aside to cool about 5 minutes. Beat egg *yolks* slightly, stir into cooled sauce mixture along with *reserved* tomato bits and mushroom slices. Pour into a 2-quart (2 liter) soufflé dish or casserole. Beat egg *whites* with cream of tartar until stiff peaks form. Fold into sauce mixture with a rubber spatula by cutting down through the center of the mixture to the bottom and sides of the dish. Fold sauce mixture over and through egg whites, just until all the sauce mixture is blended. Bake at 375° (190°C) 50 to 60 minutes. Makes 6 servings.

For lightest, puffiest savory soufflé every time: generously butter soufflé dish, dust with grated Parmesan cheese, and chill before filling.

CHEEZY TOMATO FONDUE BAKE

125 ml	½ cup melted butter
5 ml	1 teasp. garlic powder
5 ml	1 teasp. dry mustard
	1 small loaf Italian bread, cut into 1-inch (3 cm) cubes
45 ml	3 Tablesp. minced onion
8 ml	1½ teasp. salt
5 ml	1 teasp. paprika
	1 (15-oz./425 g) can Hunt's Tomato Sauce Special
750 ml	3 cups shredded Swiss cheese
85 ml	⅓ cup flour
425 ml	1⅔ cups milk
	3 eggs, beaten

Combine ¼ *cup* (60 ml) melted butter, garlic powder and ½ *teaspoon* (3 ml) dry mustard until well blended; drizzle over bread cubes in large bowl, tossing lightly. Stir *remaining* mustard, onion, salt and paprika into the Hunt's Sauce. In 2-quart (2 liter) casserole, arrange alternate layers of ⅓ *each:* bread cubes, sauce mixture and cheese, *reserving ½ cup* (125 ml) cheese. Start and end with bread cubes. In a medium saucepan, blend *remaining* butter with flour; gradually stir in milk; simmer until slightly thickened. Remove from heat. Add a little of hot mixture to eggs, stirring; gradually stir back into pan of sauce. Pour over bread cubes, let stand 1 hour. Sprinkle top with *remaining* cheese. Bake at 375° (190°C) 50 to 60 minutes or until puffy and golden on top. Makes 6 to 8 servings.

BROCCOLI 'N BEEF ROLL-UPS

Ideal for an intimate dinner

42

900 g	2 lbs.	top round steak, cut into 6 serving-size pieces
8 ml	1½ teasp.	garlic salt
1 ml	¼ teasp.	pepper
	1	(10-oz./283 g) pkg. frozen broccoli spears, thawed and drained
85 ml	⅓ cup	pure vegetable oil
125 ml	½ cup	chopped onion
	1	(8-oz./226 g) can Hunt's Tomato Sauce with Mushrooms
60 ml	¼ cup	red wine
1250 ml	5 cups	hot cooked noodles

Trim excess fat from meat; pound with meat mallet to ¼-inch (1 cm) thickness. Sprinkle with garlic salt and pepper. Top each with broccoli spears. Roll up and secure with toothpicks. Brown in oil in skillet. Add onion; sauté lightly; drain fat. Add remaining ingredients, *except* noodles. Cover; simmer 40 to 45 minutes until meat is tender. Arrange roll-ups over a bed of hot cooked noodles. Makes 4 to 6 servings.

SWEET AND SOUR CHICKEN

Succulently tender and super good

	1	(2½ to 3 lb./1200 g) broiler-fryer chicken, cut up
10 ml	2 teasp.	seasoned salt
3 ml	½ teasp.	white pepper
	1	(13-oz./368 g) can pineapple chunks
	1	(8-oz./226 g) can Hunt's Tomato Sauce
125 ml	½ cup	vinegar
60 ml	¼ cup	water
45 ml	3 Tablesp.	cornstarch
15 ml	1 Tablesp.	soy sauce
	1	chicken bouillon cube
	1	green pepper, sliced

Arrange chicken pieces in a 7½- x 12- x 1½-inch (18 x 30 x 4 cm) baking dish. Sprinkle with seasoned salt and pepper. Bake, covered, at 400° (205°C) 35 to 40 minutes. Combine remaining ingredients in medium saucepan, heat to bubbly; blend well. Pour over chicken pieces. Reduce heat to 350° (175°C); bake, uncovered, 25 to 30 minutes longer or until sauce thickens and chicken is tender. Baste once or twice. Makes 4 to 6 servings.

ELEGANT BEEF WELLINGTON DUO

The perfect dinner for two

225 g	½ lb. extra lean ground beef
125 ml	½ cup fine dry bread crumbs
	1 egg, separated
15 ml	1 Tablesp. prepared horseradish
3 ml	½ teasp. salt
1 ml	¼ teasp. monosodium glutamate
	1 (8-oz./226 g) can Hunt's Tomato Sauce
	1 pie crust stick
	Wine Sauce (recipe follows)

Combine in a medium bowl, ground beef, bread crumbs, *egg yolk,* horseradish, salt, monosodium glutamate and ¼ cup (60 ml) Hunt's Sauce. Shape mixture into 2 rectangular loaves. Bake on rack in shallow baking pan at 400° (205°C) 15 minutes. Cool on rack 5 to 10 minutes. Meanwhile, prepare pie crust stick according to package directions. Roll into 2 rectangles, large enough to wrap around loaves; place loaves in center of each pastry. Wrap pastry around, overlapping edges on bottom. Trim off excess pastry at ends. Moisten edges and pinch together to seal. Make decorative cut-outs from excess pastry and arrange on top of each loaf. Place on ungreased baking pan. Brush entire surface with *egg white* mixed with a little water. Bake at 400° (205°C) 20 minutes longer. Serve with Wine Sauce. Makes 2 servings.

Wine Sauce: Combine *remaining* Hunt's Sauce, ¼ *cup* (60 ml) wine, *2 tablespoons* (15 ml) *each:* brown sugar, lemon juice and Worcestershire and ⅛ *teaspoon* (.5 ml) crushed tarragon. Simmer over low heat about 10 minutes.

A Medley of Mexican Cooking

Mexican cuisine can change
dramatically from state to state
depending upon what kinds of foods are most
plentiful in a particular area. One
ingredient remains constant, however, and
that's tomato sauce. But, after all, the tomato
is indigenous to Mexico and its
name comes from the Aztec word, "tomatl."

In this chapter you'll find your
favorite Mexican dishes, as well
as some deliciously different ones
we're sure you'll enjoy.

Opposite: Tacos Con Pollo (page 50)

ARROLLADO

Medley of Mexican Cooking

STUFFED AND ROLLED FLANK STEAK
An authentic recipe guests and family will cheer

	1 flank steak (about 1½ lbs./675 g), butterflied*
	1 (15-oz./425 g) can Hunt's Tomato Sauce with Tomato Bits
250 ml	1 cup dry red wine
5 ml	1 teasp. garlic powder
3 ml	½ teasp. powdered thyme
	1 (10-oz./283 g) pkg. frozen chopped spinach, thawed and drained
	1 (10-oz./283 g) pkg. frozen mixed peas and carrots, cooked and drained
60 ml	¼ cup *each:* chopped green pepper, celery, onion and pimiento
30 ml	2 Tablesp. chopped parsley
5 ml	1 teasp. salt
3 ml	½ teasp. chili powder
	2 beef bouillon cubes
500 ml	2 cups cold water
10 ml	2 teasp. cornstarch

Pound steak with a meat mallet to ⅛-inch (.3 cm) thickness. Combine ½ cup (125 ml) Hunt's Sauce, wine, thyme and garlic powder in shallow baking dish; marinate flank steak in mixture about 1 hour. In a mixing bowl, toss together spinach, peas and carrots, green pepper, celery, onion, pimiento, parsley, salt, chili powder and ½ cup (125 ml) Hunt's Sauce. Drain steak, reserving marinade. Spread vegetable mixture over entire surface of steak. Starting with either cut end, roll steak jelly-roll fashion with the grain. Secure with toothpicks or kitchen string. Add *remaining* Hunt's Sauce, beef bouillon, water, and cornstarch to reserved marinade in shallow baking dish; mix well. Place stuffed meat roll in baking dish. Bake at 375° (190°C) 1 hour; baste often. Makes 4 to 8 servings.

If you partially freeze flank or round steak first, it will cut easily and neatly into strips or cubes.

***Butterfly:** Slice through the center horizontally without completely separating and spread open so as to resemble a butterfly.*

Opposite: Arrollado

PESCADO VERACRUZ^M

Medley of Mexican Cooking

FISH VERACRUZ STYLE
Red snapper cooked with a Mexican flair— olé

	1 onion, chopped
30 ml	2 Tablesp. pure vegetable oil
	1 (15-oz./425 g) can Hunt's Tomato Herb Sauce
	1 (2-oz./57 g) jar chopped pimiento
30 ml	2 Tablesp. capers
900 g	2 lbs. red snapper fillets
5 ml	1 teasp. salt
1 ml	¼ teasp. white pepper
60 ml	¼ cup sliced pimiento stuffed olives

In small skillet, sauté onion in oil. Add Hunt's Sauce, pimiento and capers. Simmer over medium heat 5 minutes. Meanwhile, place red snapper in a lightly greased shallow baking dish; sprinkle with salt and pepper. Pour sauce mixture over; top with olives. Bake at 350° (175°C) 20 to 25 minutes or until fish flakes. Makes 6 servings.

^MMicrowave

SPANISH OMELET

Medley of Mexican Cooking

Simply delicious for Sunday brunch

	4 slices bacon, cut into squares
125 ml	½ cup *each:* chopped onion and green pepper
	1 clove garlic, minced
	4 large mushrooms, sliced
	1 (8-oz./226 g) can Hunt's Tomato Sauce
3 ml	½ teasp. chili powder
	8 eggs
60 ml	¼ cup water
30 ml	2 Tablesp. butter

In a medium saucepan, sauté bacon, onion, green pepper, garlic and mushrooms until bacon is slightly crisp. Stir in Hunt's Sauce and chili powder. Simmer 3 to 5 minutes. Set aside. Beat eggs and water together in a small mixing bowl. Heat a 9- or 10-inch (23-25 cm) omelet pan or skillet over medium heat. Add *1 tablespoon* (15 ml) butter, tilting pan to coat entire surface. Add *half* the egg mixture. As omelet cooks, loosen edges with spatula and tilt pan to let uncooked portion run under until omelet is set. Spoon ½ cup (125 ml) sauce over center of omelet. Continue cooking until golden brown around edges. Loosen with spatula; slide onto serving platter, tilting pan to fold omelet in half. Spoon ½ cup (125 ml) sauce over top. Prepare second omelet as above. Makes (2 omelets) 4 servings.

Medley of Mexican Cooking **CALIFORNIA TOSTADAS**

Serve with sour cream and avocado slices

	8 corn tortillas
	Pure vegetable oil
225 ml	½ lb. *each:* ground beef and chorizo
	1 onion, chopped
	1 (8-oz./226 g) can Hunt's Tomato Sauce
	1 (30-oz./851 g) can refried beans
375 ml	1½ cups shredded Cheddar cheese
	1 head lettuce, shredded

Over medium-high heat, fry tortillas one at a time in a skillet in 1 inch (3 cm) of oil 1 to 2 minutes or until slightly crisp. Drain on paper towels. Sauté ground beef, chorizo and onion in a small skillet; drain excess fat. Add Hunt's Sauce; simmer 3 to 5 minutes. Meanwhile, heat beans thoroughly in saucepan or double boiler; stir often. To assemble tostadas, spread each tortilla with equal portions of hot beans, then with meat mixture. Sprinkle each with cheese and top with shredded lettuce. Makes 8 tostadas.

Medley of Mexican Cooking **CHILI CON CARNE**^C

The perfect meal for a cold winter day

450 g	1 lb. flank steak, cubed
	1 medium onion, quartered
	2 cloves garlic, minced
125 ml	½ cup chopped green pepper
30 ml	2 Tablesp. pure vegetable oil
	1 (15-oz./425 g) can *each:* Hunt's Tomato Sauce and Hunt's Tomato Sauce with Tomato Bits
125 ml	½ cup water
30 ml	2 Tablesp. chili powder
5 ml	1 teasp. flour
3 ml	½ teasp. *each:* salt and pepper
	1 bay leaf
3 ml	½ teasp. ground cumin
3 ml	½ teasp. diced canned jalapeno peppers
	1 (15-oz./425 g) can kidney beans

In a heavy kettle or Dutch oven, sauté steak cubes, onion, garlic and green pepper in oil until steak loses its redness. Stir in remaining ingredients, *except* kidney beans. Simmer 1½ hours; add kidney beans; simmer 30 minutes longer. Serve topped with grated Parmesan or Cheddar cheese, if desired. Makes (2 quarts/2 liters) 6 servings.

C *Slow Cooker*

TACOS CON POLLO
CHICKEN TACOS
A favorite any time of year

	1	onion, chopped
		Pure vegetable oil
875 ml	3½	cups chopped cooked chicken
	1	(8-oz./226 g) can Hunt's Tomato Sauce
125 ml	½	cup water
30 ml	2	Tablesp. chopped pimiento
15 ml	1	Tablesp. chili powder
5 ml	1	teasp. seasoned salt
3 ml	½	teasp. garlic powder
1 ml	¼	teasp. cumin
		Dash of Tabasco
	1	doz. corn tortillas
375 ml	1½	cups shredded lettuce
250 ml	1	cup shredded Cheddar cheese
180 ml	¾	cup guacamole

Sauté onion in 2 *tablespoons* (30 ml) oil in 10-inch (25 cm) skillet until transparent. Add remaining ingredients, *except* tortillas, lettuce, cheese and guacamole. Simmer over medium heat 8 to 10 minutes. Meanwhile, heat *1½ cups* oil (375 ml) to 375° (190°C) in heavy saucepan over high heat. Fold each tortilla in half. Holding with tongs, place in hot oil. Fry 2 to 3 minutes for soft shells or 3 to 5 minutes for crisp ones. Drain on paper towels. Fill each tortilla shell with equal portions of chicken mixture, lettuce, and cheese. Top with guacamole. Makes 12 tacos. (See photo page 45)

CHILIES CON QUESO
Spicy-hot and spicy-good fondue dip

	1	onion, chopped
30 ml	2	Tablesp. pure vegetable oil
	1	(4-oz./114 g) can diced green chilies
3 ml	½	teasp. salt
	1	(8-oz./226 g) can Hunt's Tomato Sauce
375 ml	1½	cups *each:* shredded Monterey Jack and Cheddar cheese

Sauté onion in oil until transparent in a 10-inch (25 cm) skillet. Add remaining ingredients. Heat over medium heat, stirring constantly, until cheese melts. Serve with tortilla chips. Makes about 3 cups (750 ml).

Note: Use a warming tray or fondue pot to keep dip warm.

Medley of Mexican Cooking

BURRITOS

Serve with sour cream or guacamole.

	1	doz. (9-inch/23 cm) flour tortillas
675 g	1½	lbs. pork shoulder cut into ½-inch (1 cm) cubes
125 ml	½	cup chopped onion
	2	cloves garlic, minced
45 ml	3	Tablesp. pure vegetable oil
	1	(15-oz./425 g) can Hunt's Tomato Sauce with Tomato Bits
	1	(20½-oz./567 g) can refried beans
.5 ml	⅛	teasp. crushed red pepper
375 ml	1½	cups shredded Cheddar or Monterey Jack cheese

Wrap tortillas in foil; heat in oven at 350° (175°C) 10 minutes. Meanwhile, sauté pork, onion and garlic in oil until pork loses its redness. Add Hunt's Sauce, refried beans and red pepper; simmer 5 to 10 minutes longer. Place equal portions in center of each warm tortilla; top with cheese. Fold sides and ends of tortilla over to enclose filling. Serve immediately. Makes 12 burritos.

Medley of Mexican Cooking

SOPA DE ALBONDIGAS[C]

MEATBALL SOUP

Great with salad, sour dough and wine

450 g	1	lb. ground beef and pork for meat loaf
	1	(15-oz./425 g) can Hunt's Tomato Sauce Special
125 ml	½	cup seasoned dry bread crumbs
	1	egg, slightly beaten
15 ml	1	Tablesp. chili powder
5 ml	1	teasp. salt
	10	pimiento stuffed olives, halved
	1	medium onion, finely chopped
	2	cloves garlic, minced
30 ml	2	Tablesp. pure vegetable oil
1 ml	¼	teasp. oregano
	2	beef bouillon cubes
875 ml	3½	cups water

In a mixing bowl, combine ground meats, ¼ *cup* (60 ml) Hunt's Sauce, bread crumbs, egg, chili powder and salt. Form into 20 (1-inch/3 cm) balls with olive half in center of each. Sauté onion and garlic in oil in heavy kettle or Dutch oven until transparent. Add *remaining* Hunt's Sauce, oregano, bouillon cubes and water. Heat to boiling. Add meatballs; reduce heat. Cover; simmer 20 to 25 minutes. Makes 6 to 8 servings.

[C]*Slow Cooker*

TAQUITOS

Great way to use cooked beef

	1	(15-oz./425 g) can Hunt's Tomato Sauce with Tomato Bits
500 ml	2	cups cubed cooked beef
30 ml	2	Tablesp. diced canned green chilies
5 ml	1	teasp. seasoned salt
3 ml	½	teasp. garlic powder
1 ml	¼	teasp. crushed red pepper
500 ml	2	cups pure vegetable oil
	1	doz. corn tortillas
		Guacamole (optional)
		Sour cream (optional)

In a 10-inch (25 cm) skillet, combine Hunt's Sauce, beef cubes, green chilies, seasoned salt, garlic powder and red pepper. Simmer 8 to 10 minutes over medium heat. Meanwhile, heat oil to 375° (190°C) in a medium saucepan over high heat. Adjust heat to maintain 375° frying temperature. Soften tortillas one at a time by dipping in and out of oil quickly. Place on paper towels. Spoon 2 to 3 tablespoons (30 to 45 ml) of meat mixture in center of each; roll up tightly; secure with toothpick. Using tongs, place rolls seam side down in 375° (190°C) oil and fry until crisp. Drain on paper towels. Serve topped with guacamole and sour cream, if desired. Makes 12 taquitos.

FRIJOLES CON CHORIZO

REFRIED BEANS

An absolute must for any Mexican meal

115 g	¼	lb. chorizo (beef or pork)
115 g	¼	lb. lean ground beef
	2	(15-oz./425 g) cans pinto beans, drained and mashed
	1	(8-oz./226 g) can Hunt's Tomato Sauce with Onions
	1	(3¾-oz./106 g) can sardines, drained (optional)
	2	corn tortillas, quartered (optional)
180 ml	¾	cup shredded sharp Cheddar cheese
30 ml	2	Tablesp. sliced ripe olives

Sauté chorizo and ground beef over high heat. Reduce heat, add beans and sauté lightly, stirring often. Stir in Hunt's Sauce and sardines; mix well. Place in a lightly greased 2-quart (2 liter) baking dish or casserole. Bake at 375° (190°C) 25 minutes. Arrange tortilla pieces over top; sprinkle with cheese and olives. Bake 5 minutes longer. Makes 6 servings.

A Medley of Mexican Cooking

ENCHILADAS^M

An exciting taste experience you can make ahead

	2 (15-oz./425 g) cans Hunt's Tomato Sauce
310 ml	1¼ cups water
25 ml	5 teasp. chili powder
10 ml	2 teasp. salt
5 ml	1 teasp. garlic powder
3 ml	½ teasp. ground cumin
	Dash of Tabasco
450 g	1 lb. ground pork and beef for meat loaf
500 ml	2 cups shredded Cheddar or Monterey Jack cheese
125 ml	½ cup sliced ripe olives
	1 doz. corn tortillas
	2 green onions, sliced

In a saucepan, combine Hunt's Sauce, water, chili powder, salt, garlic powder, cumin and Tabasco; simmer 20 minutes. Sauté meat in 10-inch (25 cm) skillet. Stir in *1½ cups* (375 ml) cheese, *1 cup* (250 ml) sauce and *¼ cup* (60 ml) olives; mix well. Spoon *¼ cup* (60 ml) sauce in 3-quart (3 liter) shallow baking dish. Soften tortillas one at a time by dipping in and out of *remaining* sauce. Spoon beef mixture down center of each tortilla; roll up, place seam side down in baking dish. Pour *remaining* sauce over top. Sprinkle with *remaining* cheese, olives and green onions. Bake at 350° (175°C) 20 minutes or until hot and bubbly. Makes 6 servings.

^M*Microwave*

A Medley of Mexican Cooking

SOPA DE LENTEJAS^C

Lentil soup for hearty appetites

250 ml	1 cup lentils
1000 ml	1 qt. water
	5 slices bacon, cut into squares
	1 medium onion, chopped
125 ml	½ cup *each:* sliced carrots and celery
	1 (15-oz./425 g) can Hunt's Tomato Sauce
5 ml	1 teasp. salt
	1 bay leaf
	3 peppercorns
	1 beef bouillon cube

Soak lentils in water 30 minutes. In a Dutch oven or heavy kettle, sauté bacon and onions until bacon is crisp and onions are transparent. Add *undrained* lentils, carrots, celery, Hunt's Sauce, salt, bay leaf, peppercorns and bouillon cube. Simmer about 1 hour. Makes 8 (1-cup/250 ml) servings.

^C*Slow Cooker*

Medley of Mexican Cooking

HUEVOS RANCHEROS
Spicy south-of-the-border breakfast dish

125 ml	½	cup chopped onion
	1	clove garlic, minced
15 ml	1	Tablesp. pure vegetable oil
	1	(8-oz./226 g) can Hunt's Tomato Sauce
60 ml	¼	cup water
	1	(2-oz./57 g) can diced green chilies
	1	beef bouillon cube
3 ml	½	teasp. *each:* oregano and pepper
	4	eggs
		Butter
	4	corn tortillas, warmed
125 ml	½	cup shredded Monterey Jack cheese
	1	avocado, sliced in crescents

Sauté onion and garlic in oil in small saucepan. Stir in Hunt's Sauce, water, green chilies, bouillon cube, oregano and pepper. Simmer 5 minutes; set aside. While sauce simmers, fry 4 eggs sunny-side up in butter. To serve, arrange eggs on a warm tortilla on serving plate. Top with equal portions of sauce, cheese and avocado crescents. Makes 4 servings.

Medley of Mexican Cooking

BIFTEC SUIZO[C]
SWISS STEAK MEXICAN STYLE
A true taste treat for hearty appetites

675 g	1½	lbs. top round, cut into 6 serving-size pieces
60 ml	¼	cup flour
5 ml	1	teasp. seasoned salt
1 ml	¼	teasp. pepper
3 ml	½	teasp. chili powder
60 ml	¼	cup pure vegetable oil
	2	cloves garlic, minced
	1	*each:* medium onion and green pepper, sliced
	1	(15-oz./425 g) can Hunt's Tomato Herb Sauce
375 ml	1½	cups water
30 ml	2	Tablesp chopped pimiento
	6	pitted black olives, halved
45 ml	3	Tablesp. sherry

Dredge meat with mixture of flour, salt, pepper and chili powder, using it all. Brown in oil in 12-inch (30 cm) skillet. Remove meat; reserve. Sauté garlic, onion and green pepper in skillet drippings until tender. Return meat to skillet, add Hunt's Sauce and water. Cover; simmer 1½ hours. Stir in pimiento, olives and sherry; simmer 10 minutes longer. Makes 6 servings.

[C] *Slow Cooker*

CHICKEN FIESTA
A fun, flavorful celebration dish   55

	1 (2½- to 3-lb./1200 g) frying chicken, cut up
	3 summer squash, sliced
	1 onion, sliced
	2 cloves garlic, minced
30 ml	2 Tablesp. pure vegetable oil
	2 ears corn, cut into 2-inch (5 cm) chunks
	1 (15-oz./425 g) can Hunt's Tomato Sauce Special
250 ml	1 cup water
250 ml	1 cup red wine
	1 bay leaf
	3 whole cloves
3 ml	½ teasp. seasoned salt
3 ml	½ teasp. cinnamon
1 ml	¼ teasp. *each:* pepper and fines herbes

Place chicken in a 9- x 13- x 1½-inch (23 x 33 x 5 cm) baking dish. Bake at 400° (205°C), uncovered, 20 minutes. Meanwhile, sauté squash, onion and garlic in oil in skillet until tender. Arrange with corn in baking dish around chicken. Combine Hunt's Sauce with *remaining* ingredients. Pour over chicken and vegetables. Cover with foil; reduce heat to 375° (190°C); bake 30 minutes longer or until chicken is tender. Makes 6 to 8 servings.

ARROZ MEXICANO
MEXICAN RICE
Side dish tradition on a Mexican menu

250 ml	1 cup uncooked rice
60 ml	¼ cup pure vegetable oil
250 ml	1 cup chopped onion
125 ml	½ cup chopped green pepper
	1 (15-oz./425 g) can Hunt's Tomato Sauce with Tomato Bits
500 ml	2 cups water
	1 beef bouillon cube
5 ml	1 teasp. salt
1 ml	¼ teasp. white pepper

In a 10-inch (25 cm) skillet, brown rice lightly in oil. Add onion and green pepper; sauté until onions are transparent. Stir in remaining ingredients; simmer, covered, over medium heat 25 to 30 minutes. Makes 4 to 6 servings.

A Medley of Mexican Cooking

OVEN EGGS WITH ZUCCHINI SALSA

An easy, economical supper or lunch

	2 medium zucchini, diagonally sliced
	Butter
	1 (8-oz./226 g) can Hunt's Tomato Sauce with Mushrooms
5 ml	1 teasp. seasoned salt
1 ml	¼ teasp. pepper
	8 eggs
125 ml	½ cup milk
250 ml	1 cup shredded Cheddar cheese
	Chopped chives or green onions

Sauté zucchini in *2 tablespoons* butter in 10-inch (25 cm) skillet. Stir in Hunt's Sauce, salt and pepper. Simmer 8 to 10 minutes. Meanwhile, slightly beat eggs with milk in medium bowl with a fork. Melt *3 tablespoons* (45 ml) butter in 8- or 9-inch (20-23 cm) baking pan. Pour in egg mixture. Bake at 350° (175°C) 10 to 15 minutes until partially cooked. Stir in *½ cup* (125 ml) cheese; bake 5 minutes longer. To serve, cut eggs into 4 individual servings. Spoon equal portions of sauce and zucchini over each. Sprinkle with chives and *remaining* cheese. Makes 4 servings.

A Medley of Mexican Cooking

NACHOS CON SALSA

A favorite Mexican appetizer no one can resist

	1 (10-oz./284 g) bag of regular toasted tortilla chips
500 ml	2 cups shredded Cheddar cheese
250 ml	1 cup Salsa (recipe follows)

Spread tortilla chips in a shallow baking pan. Sprinkle with shredded cheese. Top with salsa. Broil for 3 minutes or until cheese melts. Makes 6 to 8 servings.

SALSA

	1 (8-oz./226 g) can Hunt's Tomato Sauce
	1 (4-oz./114 g) can diced green chilies
125 ml	½ cup *each:* chopped onion and green pepper
5 ml	1 teasp. lemon juice
1 ml	¼ teasp. Tabasco

Combine ingredients in small bowl. Let stand about 30 minutes. Use as a dip for tortilla chips or as a recipe ingredient. Makes 1½ cups (375 ml).

TORTA DE GALLINA CON CHIPOTLE^M

CHIPOTLE CHICKEN

A delicious casserole you'll serve again and again

500 ml	2 cups chopped cooked chicken
30 ml	2 Tablesp. slivered almonds
30 ml	2 Tablesp. dark seedless raisins
30 ml	2 Tablesp. sliced ripe olives
	1 (15-oz./425 g) can Hunt's Tomato Sauce Special
	1 large clove garlic, minced
25 ml	1½ Tablesp. brown sugar, packed
60 ml	¼ cup vinegar
5 ml	1 teasp. paprika
5 ml	1 teasp. pure vegetable oil
3 ml	½ teasp. hickory-flavored salt
1 ml	¼ teasp. liquid smoke
.5 ml	⅛ teasp. crushed red pepper
	1 doz. corn tortillas
375 ml	1½ cups shredded Monterey Jack cheese

In a medium bowl, combine chicken, almonds, raisins and olives; toss lightly; set aside. Blend together in a small bowl, Hunt's Sauce, garlic, brown sugar, vinegar, paprika, oil, hickory salt, liquid smoke and red pepper. In a 1½-quart (1.5 liter) greased casserole, arrange alternate layers of tortillas, chicken mixture, sauce mixture and cheese, *reserving ½ cup (125 ml) cheese for top layer.* Bake at 375° (190°C) 30 to 35 minutes. Makes 6 to 8 servings.

Warm, buttered tortillas, rolled up, add to any Mexican dinner. Or make good snacking food, too.

^M*Microwave*

RECIPES TO DELIGHT THE DIETER

Dieting doesn't have to be dull. In fact,
dishes designed to help you take off those
few extra pounds can be just as delicious, just
as exciting, and just as satisfying as the
ones that aren't. In this chapter, we've
included fourteen recipes that are sure to delight
you as well as your family and friends.

They're so good, you'll want to try them
whether you're on a diet or not. Approximate
calorie counts are given for each recipe.

Opposite: Make-a-Meal Soup (page 63)

TOMATO WHIRL

41 calories per cup

	2	(8-oz./226 g) cans Hunt's Tomato Sauce
		Juice of 1 lemon
60 ml	¼	cup coarsely chopped celery leaves
60 ml	¼	cup coarsely chopped parsley
60 ml	¼	cup coarsely chopped cucumber
1 ml	¼	teasp. onion salt
1 ml	¼	teasp. Worcestershire
		Dash Tabasco
500 ml	2	cups water
	2	chicken or beef bouillon cubes (optional)

In blender container, combine *1 can* Hunt's Sauce, lemon juice, vegetables, onion salt, Worcestershire and Tabasco. Whirl in electric blender until vegetables disappear. Add *remaining can* Hunt's Sauce and water; blend. Serve chilled as a beverage *or* add bouillon cubes and heat and serve as soup for low-calorie luncheon. Makes approximately 4 cups (1 liter).

OVEN-BARBECUED CHICKEN

271 calories per serving

	1	(8-oz./226 g) can Hunt's Tomato Sauce
		with Mushrooms
60 ml	¼	cup water
15 ml	1	Tablesp. lemon juice
15 ml	1	Tablesp. brown sugar, packed
8 ml	1½	teasp. instant minced onion
5 ml	1	teasp. prepared mustard
3 ml	½	teasp. Worcestershire
.5 ml	⅛	teasp. barbecue spice
1200 g	2½	lbs. frying chicken pieces

In small bowl, combine all ingredients, *except* chicken. Blend well. Arrange chicken pieces in 7½- x 12- x 1½-inch (18 x 30 x 4 cm) baking dish. Pour sauce over chicken; cover, marinate 6 to 8 hours in refrigerator; turn occasionally. Drain chicken, *reserving* marinade. Place chicken on rack or broiler pan, skin side up. Bake at 375° (190°C) about 1 hour and 15 minutes or until tender. Baste with reserved marinade every 15 minutes during baking. Makes 4 servings.

Opposite: Oven-Barbecued Chicken

RECIPES
TO DELIGHT
THE DIETER

ZESTY FRANKS^M
159 calories per frank

450 g	1 lb. all-beef frankfurters
	1 (8-oz./226 g) can Hunt's Tomato Sauce
30 ml	2 Tablesp. vinegar
15 ml	1 Tablesp. brown sugar, packed
15 ml	1 Tablesp. prepared mustard
10 ml	2 teasp. instant minced onion
4 ml	¾ teasp. salt
3 ml	½ teasp. prepared horseradish

Score franks diagonally. Place in ungreased 6- x 10- x 1½-inch (15 x 25 x 4 cm) baking dish. In small mixing bowl, combine remaining ingredients; mix well. Pour over franks. Bake at 400° (205°C) 20 minutes; baste occasionally. Makes 10 Zesty Franks.

^M*Microwave*

RECIPES
TO DELIGHT
THE DIETER

VEAL CUTLETS ROMA
240 calories per serving

	4 (3-oz./85 g) tenderized veal cutlets
15 ml	1 Tablesp. pure vegetable oil
	1 (8-oz./226 g) can Hunt's Tomato Sauce with Cheese
125 ml	½ cup water
15 ml	1 Tablesp. minced parsley
10 ml	2 teasp. capers, drained
5 ml	1 teasp. Worcestershire
3 ml	½ teasp. dried oregano leaves
.5 ml	⅛ teasp. garlic powder

In 10-inch (25 cm) skillet, brown cutlets in oil. Drain excess fat. Blend remaining ingredients in small bowl; pour over meat. Cover, simmer 10 to 15 minutes or until cutlets are tender. To serve, spoon sauce over cutlets. Makes 4 servings.

Avoid any fad diets and, if yours is a serious weight problem, by all means consult a professional nutritionist or physician.

MAKE-A-MEAL SOUP^M

275 calories per 2 cups

450 g	1	lb. ground turkey
	1	onion, chopped
15 ml	1	Tablesp. pure vegetable oil
750 ml	3	cups water
	2	chicken bouillon cubes
5 ml	1	teasp. salt
1 ml	¼	teasp. pepper
	1	bay leaf
3 ml	½	teasp. powdered thyme
	3	*each:* carrots and celery ribs, sliced
	¼	head cabbage, cut into 1-inch (3 cm) chunks
45 ml	3	Tablesp. uncooked rice
	1	(8-oz./226 g) can Hunt's Tomato Sauce
	1	(15-oz./425 g) can red beans, undrained
	1	(28-oz./793 g) can whole tomatoes

Cook ground turkey and onion in oil in Dutch oven or large kettle until onion is tender. Add remaining ingredients. Simmer, covered, 30 minutes. Makes (14 cups/3500 ml) 6 to 8 main-dish servings. (See photo page 59)

^M*Microwave*

HALIBUT ATHENS

189 calories per serving

	1	clove garlic, minced
	1	large green pepper, cut into thin strips
	1	onion, sliced into rings
15 ml	1	Tablesp. pure vegetable oil
	1	*small* eggplant, peeled and cubed
	1	(15-oz./425 g) can Hunt's Tomato Sauce with Tomato Bits
60 ml	¼	cup sauterne wine or lemon juice
4 ml	¾	teasp. oregano
3 ml	½	teasp. seasoned salt
1200 g	2½	lbs. ¾-inch (2 cm) thick halibut steak, cut into 6 servings

In 12-inch (30 cm) skillet, sauté garlic, green pepper and onion in oil until tender. Add eggplant, Hunt's Sauce, wine or lemon juice, oregano and seasoned salt; simmer 10 minutes. Arrange halibut pieces in 9- x 13- x 2-inch (23 x 33 x 5 cm) baking dish. Spoon eggplant mixture over halibut. Bake at 425° (220°C) 12 to 15 minutes or until fish flakes easily with a fork. Spoon vegetables and sauce over fish to serve. Makes 6 servings.

RECIPES
TO DELIGHT
THE DIETER
BEEFED-UP VEGETABLE STEW
310 calories per serving

675 g	1½	lbs. lean beef chuck, cut into bite-size pieces
	2	carrots, cut into 1-inch (3 cm) pieces
	1	medium onion, sliced into rings
	1	(15-oz./425 g) can Hunt's Tomato Sauce Special
	1	beef bouillon cube, crushed
3 ml	½	teasp. salt
1 ml	¼	teasp. pepper
	4	medium zucchini, cut in half and quartered lengthwise
225 g	½	lb. mushrooms, sliced

Combine all ingredients, *except* zucchini and mushrooms, in a Dutch oven; cover. Bake at 325° (165°C) for 1½ hours. Stir in zucchini and mushrooms, cover and bake 1 hour longer or until meat is tender. Makes 6 servings.

One of the surest ways to control weight is simply to cut down size of servings . . . and resist those second helpings.

RECIPES
TO DELIGHT
THE DIETER
CHICKEN BREASTS ITALIANO[M]
218 calories per serving

	6	half chicken breasts (about 2½ lbs./1200 g), skinned
5 ml	1	teasp. salt
.5 ml	⅛	teasp. pepper
	1	(15-oz./425 g) can Hunt's Tomato Herb Sauce

Arrange skinned chicken breasts in 9- x 13- x 2-inch (23 x 33 x 5 cm) baking pan. Sprinkle with salt and pepper. Pour Hunt's Sauce over chicken. Bake at 350° (175°C) 1 hour or until chicken is tender. Makes 6 servings.

[M]*Microwave*

RECIPES
TO DELIGHT
THE DIETER

THICK-'N-CREAMY LO-CAL DRESSING

17 calories per 2 tablespoons (30 ml)   65

	1 (15-oz./425 g) can Hunt's Tomato Sauce Special
250 ml	1 cup small curd cottage cheese
60 ml	¼ to ½ cup water
15 ml	1 Tablesp. lemon juice
8 ml	1½ teasp. instant minced onion
6 ml	1¼ teasp. salt
5 ml	1 teasp. dry mustard
3 ml	½ teasp. basil
.5 ml	⅛ teasp. pepper

Combine all ingredients in blender container. Blend on high speed until completely smooth. Chill thoroughly. Refrigerate unused portion tightly covered. Makes about 3 cups (750 ml).

RECIPES
TO DELIGHT
THE DIETER

SHRIMP CREOLE

108 calories per serving

	1 onion, thinly sliced
	1 rib celery, chopped
	1 small green pepper, minced
	1 clove garlic, crushed
15 ml	1 Tablesp. pure vegetable oil
15 ml	1 Tablesp. flour
30 ml	2 Tablesp. water
3 ml	½ teasp. chili powder
	1 (15-oz./425 g) can Hunt's Tomato Sauce
3 ml	½ teasp. salt
500 ml	2 cups (about 12 ozs./340 g) small cooked, cleaned shrimp

In 10-inch (25 cm) skillet, sauté vegetables and garlic in oil until tender. Make a paste of the flour and water. Add this mixture, the chili powder, Hunt's Sauce and salt to the vegetables. Simmer, stirring occasionally, 10 minutes. Add the shrimp; simmer 5 minutes longer. Makes 6 servings.

RECIPES
TO DELIGHT
THE DIETER

TURKEY ORIENTAL^M

231 calories per serving

250 ml	1 cup sliced mushrooms
250 ml	1 cup sliced celery
60 ml	¼ cup chopped onion
15 ml	1 Tablesp. pure vegetable oil
500 ml	2 cups cubed cooked turkey
	1 (15-oz./425 g) can Hunt's Tomato Sauce with Tomato Bits
	1 (16-oz./454 g) can bean sprouts, drained
30 ml	2 Tablesp. soy sauce
60 ml	¼ cup water
15 ml	1 Tablesp. cornstarch

Sauté mushrooms, celery and onion in oil in 10-inch (25 cm) skillet until onion is tender. Add turkey, Hunt's Sauce, bean sprouts and soy sauce. Simmer 10 minutes. Blend water and cornstarch. Add to skillet. Cook, stirring constantly, until mixture comes to a boil and thickens. Makes 4 servings.

^M*Microwave*

RECIPES
TO DELIGHT
THE DIETER

MINI PIZZAS

129 calories per serving

	2 (6-inch/15 cm) rounds of pita or Arabic flat bread
	1 (8-oz./226 g) can Hunt's Tomato Sauce with Mushrooms
3 ml	½ teasp. Italian herb seasoning
1 ml	¼ teasp. oregano
	Dash garlic powder
250 ml	1 cup shredded low-moisture, part-skim mozzarella cheese

Carefully separate each piece of pita bread into 2 layers to form "pizza crusts." Place, crust side down, on cookie sheet. Spread ¼ of the Hunt's Sauce on cut side of each "pizza" crust. Sprinkle *each* with ¼ of the Italian herb seasoning mixed with oregano and garlic powder. Top *each* with ¼ *cup* (60 ml) cheese. Bake at 450° (230°C) 10 minutes. Makes 4 servings.

RECIPES TO DELIGHT THE DIETER

CRAB-IN-TOMATO ASPIC

67 calories per serving

	2	envelopes (2 Tablesp./30 ml) unflavored gelatine
375 ml	1½	cups water
	1	(6-oz./170 g) pkg. frozen crabmeat, thawed
	2	(8-oz./226 g) cans Hunt's Tomato Sauce with Onions
	2	beef bouillon cubes
	1	bay leaf
1 ml	¼	teasp. celery salt
30 ml	2	Tablesp. lemon juice
250 ml	1	cup chopped celery

Soften gelatine in ½ *cup* (125 ml) water, set aside. Drain crab, reserving liquid. In medium saucepan, combine crab liquid, *remaining 1 cup* water (250 ml), Hunt's Sauce, bouillon cubes, bay leaf and celery salt; bring to a boil. Remove bay leaf. Add softened gelatine and lemon juice; stir until gelatine is dissolved. Chill until mixture is slightly thickened. Fold in celery and crabmeat. Turn into 6-cup (1.5 liter) mold; chill until firm. Unmold on bed of greens. Makes 6 servings.

RECIPES TO DELIGHT THE DIETER

PEPPER STEAK

284 calories per serving without *rice*

450 g	1	lb. round steak, ½ inch (1 cm) thick, with all fat removed
15 ml	1	Tablesp. pure vegetable oil
	1	(15-oz./425 g) can Hunt's Tomato Sauce with Tomato Bits
	½	medium onion, thinly sliced
	1	small clove garlic, minced
	2	beef bouillon cubes
	1	large green pepper, cut into ¼-inch (.5 cm) strips

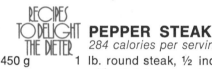

Don't cut out all carbohydrates—just know the calorie count. A baked potato is 90, ½ cup steamed rice, 110. It's what you put on top that counts.

Cut round steak into 2- x ¼-inch (5 x .5 cm) strips. In 10-inch (25 cm) skillet, brown steak strips in oil; drain fat. Add Hunt's Sauce, onion slices, garlic and bouillon cubes. Cover tightly and simmer 30 minutes. Add green pepper strips. Simmer, uncovered, 10 minutes longer or until green pepper is crisp-tender. Serve over rice, if desired. Makes 4 servings.

COLORFUL ITALIAN CUISINE

When one thinks of Italian
cuisine, one immediately thinks of
tomatoes. But the fact of the matter is,
the tomato wasn't introduced to
Italy until the sixteenth century, when it
was brought from the New World.

This chapter has a marvelous
collection of twenty-two recipes,
a sampling of Italian cooking that
embraces everything from the rich foods
of the north, the robust foods of
the Romans, to the spicy foods
of the south. Buon gusto!

Opposite: Mamma Mia Pizza (page 72)

COLORFUL ITALIAN CUISINE

EGGPLANT PARMIGIANA
Great way to serve economical eggplant

	1 large eggplant
125 ml	½ cup pure vegetable oil
	1 (15-oz./425 g) can Hunt's Tomato Sauce with Tomato Bits
	1 clove garlic, minced
5 ml	1 teasp. oregano
225 g	½ lb. shredded mozzarella cheese
	2 pepperoni sticks (about 5 oz./142 g), sliced
60 ml	¼ cup grated Parmesan cheese

Peel eggplant; cut into ½-inch-thick (1 cm) slices. In 12-inch (30 cm) skillet, brown in oil. Combine Hunt's Sauce, garlic and oregano. Arrange *half* the eggplant slices in 7½- x 12- x 1½-inch (18 x 30 x 4 cm) baking dish; pour *half* the sauce mixture over, sprinkle with *half* the mozarella and layer with *half* the pepperoni. Repeat layers. Top with Parmesan. Bake at 350° (175°C) 30 minutes. Makes 6 servings.

COLORFUL ITALIAN CUISINE

FISH RIPIENI
Elegant stuffed fish that's easy to do

125 ml	½ cup *each:* minced onion and celery
	Butter
375 ml	1½ cups seasoned stuffing mix
250 ml	1 cup water
30 ml	2 Tablesp. chopped parsley
	1 (2-oz./56 g) can anchovies, chopped (optional)
900 g	2 lbs. whole or piece of codfish or halibut, 1 inch (3 cm) thick
	Salt and pepper
	1 (15-oz./425 g) can Hunt's Tomato Sauce Special
5 ml	1 teasp. capers

Sauté onion and celery in ¼ cup (60 ml) butter. Add stuffing mix, ½ cup (125 ml) water, parsley and anchovies. Blend well. Sprinkle fish with salt and pepper. Cut pocket in middle of fish. Fill with stuffing. Place in 9- x 13- x 2-inch (23 x 33 x 5 cm) baking dish. Brush with about 2 *tablespoons* (30 ml) melted butter. Combine Hunt's Sauce, capers and ½ cup (125 ml) water. Pour over top and around edges of fish. Bake at 400° (205°C) 20 to 25 minutes. Makes 6 servings.

Opposite: Fish Ripieni

MAMMA MIA PIZZA
Pizza never tasted so good

875 ml	3½ to 4	cups sifted all-purpose flour
	2	pkgs. active dry yeast
375 ml	1½	cups water
		Olive or pure vegetable oil
13 ml	2½	teasp. salt
		Pizza Sauce (recipe follows)
750 ml	3	cups shredded mozzarella, jack or Cheddar cheese
		Toppings*

For a short-cut pizza yeast dough crust, use a package of roll mix or frozen bread dough.

In large mixer bowl, combine *2 cups* (500 ml) flour and yeast. Blend water, *3 tablespoons* (45 ml) oil and salt; heat to lukewarm (120 to 130°/49 to 55°C). Add to flour mixture; beat on medium speed 3 minutes. Stir in *1½ to 2 cups* (375 to 500 ml) *more* flour to make a stiff dough. Knead on floured board until smooth. Place in greased bowl; turn once to grease entire surface. Cover and let rise (about 1 hour) until double. Punch down; let rest 10 minutes. Form into 2 balls. Roll each to fit a 15-inch (38 cm) pizza or jelly roll pan. Place in pans and form edges. Prick crusts. Bake at 450° (230°C) 15 to 20 minutes. Spread Pizza Sauce over surfaces. Sprinkle with shredded cheese, add desired toppings and drizzle *1 to 2 tablespoons* (15 to 30 ml) olive oil over all. Bake 10 minutes longer. Makes two (15-inch/38 cm) pizzas. (See photo page 69)

*Toppings: prosciutto ham, pepperoni, salami, Italian sausage, tiny meatballs, anchovies, shrimp, capers, green pepper strips, onion rings, garlic slivers, mushrooms, tuna.

PIZZA SAUCE
Pizza lovers . . . keep this sauce on hand   73

45 ml	3	Tablesp. olive or pure vegetable oil
250 ml	1	cup finely chopped onion
15 ml	1	Tablesp. finely chopped garlic
	2	(15-oz./425 g) cans Hunt's Tomato Sauce with Tomato Bits
180 ml	¾	cup water
15 ml	1	Tablesp. oregano
15 ml	1	Tablesp. salt
10 ml	2	teasp. sugar
5 ml	1	teasp. basil
	1	bay leaf
		Dash pepper

In a 3-quart (3 liter) saucepan, heat oil and sauté onion until golden. Add garlic and cook 1 or 2 minutes longer, stirring. Add remaining ingredients and simmer slowly, uncovered, for about 1 hour or until thick. Remove bay leaf. Use *half* the sauce to make 2 (15-inch/38 cm) pizzas. Freeze remainder. Makes about 1 quart (1 liter) sauce.

RISOTTO WITH SHRIMP
An authentic dish that's easy on the cook

30 ml	2	Tablesp. pure vegetable oil
	1	onion, chopped
125 ml	½	cup chopped green pepper
375 ml	1½	cups uncooked rice
	1	(15-oz./425 g) can Hunt's Tomato Sauce with Tomato Bits
	1	(10-oz./305 g) can chicken broth
5 ml	1	teasp. salt
3 ml	½	teasp. basil
1 ml	¼	teasp. pepper
	8	ozs. (2 cups/500 ml) cooked shrimp
125 ml	½	cup cooked peas

Heat oil in a large skillet that has a tight lid. Sauté onion, green pepper and rice until golden. Add remaining ingredients, *except* shrimp and peas. Cover; cook over very low heat, without raising lid, for 30 minutes. Stir in shrimp and peas. Cover and heat 10 minutes. Makes 4 to 6 servings.

COLORFUL ITALIAN CUISINE # EASY ZUCCHINI SAUSAGE BAKE
A budget stretcher with eye appeal

225 g	½	lb. Italian sausage
125 ml	½	cup chopped onion
	3	zucchini, cut into ½-inch (1 cm) slices
	1	(15-oz./425 g) can Hunt's Tomato Herb Sauce
750 ml	3	cups hot cooked rice
5 ml	1	teasp. seasoned salt
125 ml	½	cup shredded mozzarella cheese
60 ml	¼	cup grated Parmesan cheese

Remove sausage from casing; cook with onion in 10-inch
(25 cm) skillet until sausage loses redness. Remove and drain
on paper towel. Sauté zucchini in skillet drippings until
transparent. Cover; cook 5 minutes or until almost done;
reserve. Combine *half* the Hunt's Sauce with rice and sausage
mixture in 7½- x 12- x 1½-inch (18 x 30 x 4 cm) baking dish.
Add salt; mix well. Arrange slices of zucchini over top.
Sprinkle with mozzarella and Parmesan; spoon *remaining*
Hunt's Sauce over all. Bake, *covered,* at 350° (175°C) 20
minutes. Makes 4 to 6 servings.

COLORFUL ITALIAN CUISINE # CHICKEN CACCIATORE
An old-world favorite

60 ml	¼	cup flour
		Salt and pepper
1200 g	2½	to 3 lbs. frying chicken pieces
60 ml	¼	cup pure vegetable oil
250 ml	1	cup chopped onion
250 ml	1	cup chopped green pepper
	1	(15-oz./425 g) can Hunt's Tomato Sauce with Tomato Bits
250 ml	1	cup water
	1	(4-oz./114 g) can sliced mushrooms, drained
10 ml	2	teasp. oregano
8 ml	1½	teasp. salt
5 ml	1	teasp. sugar
3 ml	½	teasp. garlic powder
.5 ml	⅛	teasp. black pepper

Season flour with salt and pepper; use to coat chicken. In
12-inch (30 cm) skillet, brown coated chicken in oil. Remove,
drain on paper towels. Add onion and green pepper to skillet;
cook until onion is soft. Drain excess fat. Add remaining
ingredients. Blend well. Return chicken to skillet. Cover, simmer
45 minutes. Makes 6 servings.

COLORFUL ITALIAN CUISINE

CANNELLONI

For a gourmet touch, substitute crêpes for manicotti shells

250 ml	1 cup thick prepared or canned white sauce
125 ml	½ cup grated Parmesan cheese
	1 egg yolk
225 g	8 ozs. ricotta cheese
125 ml	½ cup diced Italian salami
125 ml	½ cup shredded mozzarella cheese
30 ml	2 Tablesp. chopped parsley
	10 manicotti shells
	1 (15-oz./425 g) can Hunt's Tomato Herb Sauce
125 ml	½ cup water
5 ml	1 teasp. fines herbes

In medium bowl, combine white sauce, ¼ *cup* (60 ml) Parmesan, egg yolk, ricotta, salami, mozzarella and parsley. Blend well, set aside. Cook manicotti shells in boiling salted water to cover for 5 minutes. Rinse in cold water; drain. Fill with equal portions of salami and cheese mixture. Combine Hunt's Sauce, water and fines herbes. Pour *half* in 7½- x 12 x 1½-inch (18 x 30 x 4 cm) baking dish. Arrange filled manicotti shells in sauce. Pour *remaining* sauce mixture over all. Cover, bake at 375° (190°C) 35 to 40 minutes. Sprinkle with *remaining* Parmesan. Makes 5 servings.

COLORFUL ITALIAN CUISINE

VEAL PARMESAN

A successful favorite every single time

450 g	1 lb. veal steak or minute steak
	Salt and pepper
	1 egg
60 ml	¼ cup grated Parmesan cheese
60 ml	¼ cup fine dry bread crumbs
60 ml	¼ cup pure vegetable oil
	1 (8-oz./226 g) can Hunt's Tomato Sauce with Onions
	1 clove garlic, minced
3 ml	½ teasp. marjoram
225 g	½ lb. mozzarella or Swiss cheese, sliced

Cut veal into 6 or 8 pieces. Sprinkle with salt and pepper. Beat egg with *2 teaspoons* (10 ml) water. Dip veal in egg, coat with Parmesan tossed with bread crumbs. Heat oil in large skillet. Sauté veal until golden brown on each side. Add Hunt's Sauce, garlic and marjoram. Simmer, covered, 30 minutes. Top with cheese slices last five minutes. Makes 4 servings.

COLORFUL ITALIAN CUISINE

SUNNY AND BRIGHT POLENTA PIE

A buffet masterpiece that's a meal in itself

375 ml	1½	cups yellow cornmeal
		Water
10 ml	2	teasp. salt
	2	eggs, beaten
125 ml	½	cup shredded Cheddar cheese
10 ml	2	teasp. paprika
450 g	1	lb. lean ground beef
	1	medium onion, chopped
	2	cloves garlic, minced
	1	(15-oz./425 g) can Hunt's Tomato Herb Sauce
	1	(9- to 10-oz./283 g) pkg. frozen Italian green beans or baby lima beans, thawed and drained
125 ml	½	cup grated Parmesan cheese

In bowl, combine cornmeal with *1 cup* (250 ml) cold water and *1 teaspoon* (5 ml) salt. Add to *3 cups* (750 ml) boiling water in saucepan. Cook over medium heat for 15 minutes; stir frequently to prevent sticking. Remove from heat and let cool a few minutes. Quickly stir in eggs, Cheddar cheese and paprika; spread *half* of mixture on bottom and up sides of greased round 2-quart (2 liter) glass casserole dish; set aside. Cook beef with onion and garlic in skillet until meat loses redness; drain fat. Stir in Hunt's Sauce, *remaining* salt, green beans and Parmesan cheese. Turn meat mixture into casserole and spread top with *remaining* cornmeal mixture. Bake at 375° (190°C) 1 hour. Let stand 10 minutes. Run metal spatula around edges of casserole and carefully unmold pie onto serving plate. If desired, garnish with ripe olives, carrot curls, chopped parsley and watercress. Slice into wedges to serve. Makes 6 servings.

OLD-COUNTRY POT ROAST AND SPAGHETTI

The pot roast cooks right in the sauce

	1 (2-lb./900 g) chuck pot roast, 2 inches (5 cm) thick
	1 clove garlic, slivered
30 ml	2 Tablesp. pure vegetable oil
30 ml	2 Tablesp. butter or margarine
	1 clove garlic, minced
	1 small onion, chopped
10 ml	2 teasp. oregano
5 ml	1 teasp. thyme
5 ml	1 teasp. salt
1 ml	¼ teasp. pepper
.5 ml	⅛ teasp. cinnamon
	2 (15-oz./425 g) cans Hunt's Tomato Sauce
250 ml	1 cup water
450 g	1 lb. spaghetti, cooked and drained
	Grated Parmesan cheese

Make 4 slits in roast and insert garlic slivers. Heat oil and butter in large kettle or Dutch oven. Brown meat on all sides. Remove meat. Add *minced* garlic, onion and seasonings; sauté until onion is soft. Add Hunt's Sauce and water and return meat to kettle. Bring to boil and simmer, covered, about 2 hours until tender; turn meat occasionally. Slice meat. Skim fat from sauce and serve over spaghetti with meat alongside. Sprinkle all with Parmesan. Makes 6 servings.

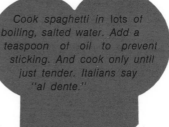

Cook spaghetti in lots of boiling, salted water. Add a teaspoon of oil to prevent sticking. And cook only until just tender. Italians say "al dente."

SPAGHETTINI BOLOGNESE
This king of spaghetti comes from Bologna

115 g	¼ lb. mushrooms, sliced
	1 carrot, sliced
	1 clove garlic, crushed
125 ml	½ cup *each:* chopped onion, celery and green pepper
30 ml	2 Tablesp. pure vegetable oil
350 g	¾ lb. Italian sausage, casings removed
	2 (15-oz./425 g) cans Hunt's Tomato Sauce
125 ml	½ cup water
60 ml	¼ cup dry red wine
5 ml	1 teasp. sugar
1 ml	¼ teasp. Italian seasoning
350 g	12 ozs. spaghettini or spaghetti, cooked and drained

Sauté mushrooms, carrot, garlic, onion, celery and green pepper in oil in Dutch oven. Add sausage; cook until sausage loses its redness. Drain fat. Add remaining ingredients. Simmer, uncovered, 30 to 40 minutes, stirring occasionally. Serve over hot, cooked spaghettini or spaghetti. Makes 4 to 6 servings.

CAPONATA
ANTIPASTO VEGETABLE RELISH
A first course perfect for a buffet dish, too

60 ml	¼ cup pure vegetable oil
	1 medium onion, sliced
	1 green pepper, cut into strips
250 ml	1 cup sliced celery
250 ml	1 cup *each of two:* eggplant cubes, small whole mushrooms, sliced zucchini, cauliflowerets
	1 (15-oz./425 g) can Hunt's Tomato Herb Sauce
30 ml	2 Tablesp. vinegar
15 ml	1 Tablesp. sugar
15 ml	1 Tablesp. capers (optional)
15 ml	1 Tablesp. chopped parsley
5 ml	1 teasp. salt
1 ml	¼ teasp. pepper
	12 whole pitted ripe olives

In a 10-inch (25 cm) skillet, heat oil; sauté vegetables 10 minutes. Add remaining ingredients, *except* olives, and simmer, uncovered, 10 minutes. Chill. Serve on a lettuce leaf and garnish with olives and crackers. Makes 6 to 8 servings.

MINESTRONE

An extra-super soup that's worth the effort

	1 clove garlic, minced
500 ml	2 cups chopped onion
250 ml	1 cup chopped celery
60 ml	¼ cup chopped parsley
60 ml	¼ cup pure vegetable oil
	3 (8-oz./226 g) cans Hunt's Tomato Sauce
	1 (10½-oz./298 g) can beef broth
1750 ml	7 cups water
	1 head of cabbage, coarsely chopped
	2 carrots, thinly sliced
15 ml	1 Tablesp. salt
1 ml	¼ teasp. pepper
1 ml	¼ teasp. sage
	1 (1-lb./450 g) can kidney beans, undrained
	1 zucchini squash, thinly sliced
250 ml	1 cup green beans or peas
250 ml	1 cup elbow macaroni
	Grated Parmesan cheese

In a large pot, sauté garlic, onion, celery and parsley in oil until soft. Stir in Hunt's Sauce and next 7 ingredients. Stir and bring to boil. Lower heat, cover and simmer slowly 1 hour. Add kidney beans and remaining ingredients, *except* cheese. Cook 10 to 15 minutes longer or until macaroni is tender. Serve topped with grated Parmesan. Makes 8 to 10 servings.

Spaghetti and macaroni double in volume during cooking. Noodles remain about the same.

COLORFUL ITALIAN CUISINE
ITALIAN CHICKEN IN WHITE WINE
A wine-lover's casserole delight

900 g	2 to 2½ lbs. frying chicken, cut up
	Salt and pepper
60 ml	4 Tablesp. butter or margarine
	1 onion, finely chopped
	2 (8-oz./226 g) cans Hunt's Tomato Sauce with Mushrooms
30 ml	2 Tablesp. chopped parsley
3 ml	½ teasp. thyme
	1 bay leaf
	1 (10½-oz./298 g) can chicken broth
250 ml	1 cup white wine
375 ml	1½ cups uncooked rice

Dry chicken thoroughly on paper towels. Season with salt and pepper and brown chicken pieces in butter or margarine in 10-inch (25 cm) skillet; remove. Add onion to skillet; sauté until soft. Add Hunt's Sauce and remaining ingredients. Heat to boil. Pour into 9- x 13- x 1½-inch (23 x 33 x 4 cm) baking dish, arrange chicken pieces in single layer in mixture. Cover and bake at 350° (175°C) 30 minutes. Remove cover; bake 15 minutes longer or until rice is tender. Makes 4 servings.

COLORFUL ITALIAN CUISINE
BAKED STUFFED TUFALI
A unique Italian way to cook ground beef

125 ml	½ cup grated Parmesan cheese
450 g	1 lb. lean ground beef
3 ml	½ teasp. salt
.5 ml	⅛ teasp. pepper
15 ml	1 Tablesp. chopped parsley
	2 eggs, beaten
225 g	½ lb. tufali, large shell macaroni or manicotti
	Marinara Sauce (recipe follows)

Combine 2 *tablespoons* (30 ml) cheese with all ingredients, *except* pasta and Marinara Sauce. Pour boiling water over pasta to completely cover and let stand 5 minutes; drain and rinse. Stuff with meat mixture. Pour *half* the Marinara Sauce in a 13- x 9- x 2-inch (33 x 23 x 5 cm) baking dish. Arrange stuffed pasta in sauce and pour *remaining* sauce over to cover. Sprinkle with *remaining* cheese. Bake at 350° (175°C) 35 to 45 minutes. Makes 4 to 6 servings.

MARINARA SAUCE
The perfect all-purpose Italian sauce   81

125 ml	½ cup chopped onion
125 ml	½ cup chopped celery
	1 clove garlic, minced
30 ml	2 Tablesp. pure vegetable oil
	2 (15-oz./425 g) cans Hunt's Tomato Sauce Special
60 ml	¼ cup red wine
3 ml	½ teasp. basil
3 ml	½ teasp. oregano
3 ml	½ teasp. salt
1 ml	¼ teasp. pepper
	1 bay leaf

In a medium saucepan, sauté onion, celery and garlic in oil. Add remaining ingredients and simmer 15 minutes. Makes 1 quart (1 liter) sauce.

Note: Simmer 10 minutes longer to serve over hot cooked pasta.

LASAGNA
Sensational dish for family and friends

450 g	1 lb. lean ground beef
	1 onion, chopped
	2 cloves garlic, minced
15 ml	1 Tablesp. minced parsley
10 ml	2 teasp. salt
3 ml	½ teasp. basil
1 ml	¼ teasp. fennel seed
.5 ml	⅛ teasp. ground cumin
	3 (8-oz./226 g) cans Hunt's Tomato Sauce
225 g	8 ozs. ricotta or cottage cheese
	2 eggs
225 g	8 ozs. lasagna noodles, cooked
350 g	¾ lb. mozzarella cheese, sliced
60 ml	¼ cup grated Parmesan cheese

In a skillet, brown ground beef with onions, garlic and seasonings; pour off fat. Stir in Hunt's Sauce; simmer 10 minutes. Meanwhile, blend ricotta and eggs. In 13- x 9- x 2-inch (33 x 23 x 5 cm) baking dish spread ¼ *cup* (60 ml) meat sauce in thin layer; add layer of *half* the noodles, *all* the ricotta mixture and *half* the mozzarella. Cover cheese layer with *half* the meat sauce and all *remaining* noodles. Top with *remaining* meat sauce and mozzarella. Sprinkle with Parmesan. Bake at 350° (175°C) 30 minutes. Let stand 10 minutes before cutting. Makes 8 servings.

COLORFUL ITALIAN CUISINE

BEEF BRACIOLA

A little extra effort makes this a memorable meal

900 g	2	lbs. top round steak
		Garlic salt
	16	slices Italian dry salami
375 ml	1½	cups shredded mozzarella cheese
45 ml	3	Tablesp. pure vegetable oil
	1	(15-oz./425 g) can Hunt's Tomato Herb Sauce
170 ml	⅔	cup canned beef broth
125 ml	½	cup dry white wine
5 ml	1	teasp. sugar
	1	bay leaf
3 ml	½	teasp. oregano
1 ml	¼	teasp. thyme
250 ml	1	cup thinly sliced zucchini
	1	(10-oz./283 g) pkg. fettuccine or egg noodles, cooked and drained

Trim fat from beef; pound with meat mallet to ⅛-inch (.5 cm) thickness. Sprinkle with garlic salt. Cut into 8 pieces. Top with salami and mozzarella. Roll up and secure with toothpicks. Brown in oil in 10-inch (25 cm) skillet; drain fat. Combine remaining ingredients, *except* zucchini and fettuccine; mix well. Pour over meat rolls. Cover; simmer 1½ hours. Add zucchini. Cover; simmer 30 minutes longer. Arrange meat rolls and zucchini on bed of fettuccine. Thicken skillet juices and serve with meat rolls. Makes 4 to 6 servings.

COLORFUL ITALIAN CUISINE

MOSTACCIOLI MILANO

A simple dish that tastes simply divine

	2	carrots, thinly sliced
	1	clove garlic, crushed
125 ml	½	cup sliced celery
125 ml	½	cup chopped onion
45 ml	3	Tablesp. minced parsley
30 ml	2	Tablesp. vegetable oil
450 g	1	lb. chicken livers
	2	(8-oz./226 g) or 1 (15-oz./425 g) can Hunt's Tomato Sauce
	1	(2-oz./56 g) can sliced mushrooms, undrained
30 ml	2	Tablesp. white wine
3 ml	½	teasp. salt
225 g	8	ozs. mostaccioli or spaghetti, cooked and drained
		Grated Parmesan cheese

Sauté carrots, garlic, celery, onion and parsley in oil in 10-inch (25 cm) skillet. Add chicken livers; cook until they lose redness. Add Hunt's Sauce, mushrooms, wine and salt. Bring to a boil. Cover; simmer 20 to 25 minutes. Stir occasionally. Spoon over mostaccioli. Sprinkle with Parmesan. Makes 4 to 5 servings.

SPAGHETTI 'N MEATBALLS DA VINCI

Sixteen magical meatballs from one half pound of beef

225 g	½	lb. lean ground beef
500 ml	2	cups soft bread crumbs
180 ml	¾	cup finely chopped, roasted peanuts
60 ml	¼	cup finely chopped onion
	2	eggs
60 ml	¼	cup non-fat dry milk
3 ml	½	teasp. salt
1 ml	¼	teasp. pepper
60 ml	¼	cup vegetable oil
	2	(15-oz./425 g) cans Hunt's Tomato Sauce
250 ml	1	cup water
5 ml	1	teasp. oregano
	1	clove garlic, crushed
5 ml	1	teasp. sugar
	1	beef bouillon cube
		Hot cooked spaghetti
		Grated Parmesan cheese

Combine first 8 ingredients. Shape into 16 meatballs. Brown in oil in large skillet; pour off fat. Stir in Hunt's Sauce and remaining ingredients, *except* spaghetti and Parmesan; simmer, covered, 30 minutes. Serve over hot cooked spaghetti. Sprinkle with cheese. Makes 4 to 6 servings.

Stretch your meat budget dollar by making less meat go further with the addition of other high protein foods like nuts, non-fat dry milk and eggs.

Convenient One-Dish Meals

Cooking can be fun or a real
chore. Meals can be interesting or a
terrible bore. But serve a delicious new
casserole, a special soup or stew, or a
quick stove-top main dish and dinner is
seldom a chore and never a bore.

This chapter brings you over twenty
of these most-sought-after
recipes. With a salad and a simple dessert,
your main dish becomes a whole meal.

Opposite: Traditional Stew Pot (page 92)

Convenient One-Dish Meals
ITALIAN CHICKEN CASSEROLE
Tastes like you slaved all day

1350 g	1	(3-lb.) frying chicken, cut up
		Salt and pepper
60 ml	¼	cup pure vegetable oil
125 ml	½	cup chopped onion
60 ml	¼	cup chopped green pepper
	1	clove garlic, minced
	3	carrots, sliced
	1	rib celery, sliced
	1	(15-oz./425 g) can Hunt's Tomato Herb Sauce
375 ml	1½	cups water
3 ml	½	teasp. basil
375 ml	1½	cups elbow or corkscrew macaroni, blanched
60 ml	¼	cup grated Parmesan cheese

Sprinkle chicken with salt and pepper. Brown in oil in skillet and remove. Lightly sauté onion, green pepper and garlic in skillet drippings. Add remaining ingredients, *except* macaroni and Parmesan; simmer 10 minutes. Put macaroni in greased 7½ x 12 x 1½-inch (18 x 30 x 4 cm) baking dish. Arrange chicken over top. Pour sauce mixture over all. Cover; bake at 350° (175°C) 45 minutes. Sprinkle with Parmesan; bake, uncovered, 10 minutes longer. Makes 4 servings.

Convenient One-Dish Meals
PORK CHOPS AND RICE INDIENNE
A favorite combination with an elegant touch

	4	center-cut pork chops, ½ inch (1 cm) thick
30 ml	2	Tablesp. pure vegetable oil
		Salt and pepper
	1	(6-oz./170 g) pkg. long grain and wild rice with herbs and seasonings
	1	(10-oz./283 g) can beef consommé
	1	(15-oz./425 g) can Hunt's Tomato Sauce Special
60 ml	¼	cup golden seedless raisins
	4	thin slices onion
	4	thin rings of green pepper
60 ml	¼	cup chopped salted peanuts

In 10-inch (25 cm) skillet, brown pork chops in oil on each side; sprinkle with salt and pepper. Remove. Add rice and seasoning packet, consommé, Hunt's Sauce and raisins. Blend well. Arrange pork chops on rice; top with onion slices and green pepper rings. Cover; simmer 45 minutes. Sprinkle peanuts over top before serving. Makes 4 servings.

Opposite: Pork Chops and Rice Indienne

Convenient One-Dish Meals

HUNT'S BURGERONI
Convenient crowd-pleaser you can count on

750 ml	3	cups shell macaroni
30 ml	2	Tablesp. butter or margarine
60 ml	¼	cup chopped chives or green onions
250 ml	1	cup diced Cheddar cheese
675 g	1½	lbs. extra-lean ground beef
		Salt and pepper
	2	(15-oz./425 g) or 1 (29-oz./822 g) can Hunt's Tomato Sauce
250 ml	1	cup water
10 ml	2	to 3 teasp. chili powder
3 ml	½	teasp. sugar
	1	(3½-oz./98 g) French-fried onions

Cook macaroni in boiling salted water according to directions on package, drain; toss with butter and chives and arrange in bottom of a 9- x 13- x 1½-inch (23 x 33 x 4 cm) baking dish. Sprinkle on the cheese; then crumble ground beef in a layer over all. Sprinkle with salt and pepper. Pour over Hunt's Sauce mixed with water, chili powder and sugar. Cover; bake at 375° (190°C) 35 to 40 minutes. Remove cover; top with onion rings and bake 10 minutes longer. Makes 8 to 10 servings.*

*For 4 to 6 servings; prepare in 2 (6- x 10- x 1½-inch/15 x 25 x 4 cm) casseroles. Bake one as directed above; freeze the other for later use.

Convenient One-Dish Meals

BACHELOR PARTY BEAN BAKE[C]
Backyard party winner every time

750 ml	3	cups large dried lima beans
		Water
8 ml	1½	teasp. salt
675 g	1½	lbs. link sausages, cut into chunks (pork, smokie and/or Polish)
	2	(8-oz./226 g) cans Hunt's Tomato Sauce with Onions
250 ml	1	cup beer
30 ml	2	Tablesp. brown sugar, packed
5 ml	1	teasp. dry mustard
	2	cloves garlic, minced

Rinse beans, cover with boiling water; cover, let stand 1 hour. Add salt, *enough more water* to cover beans; boil slowly, uncovered, 1 hour; drain. Meanwhile, brown sausages in large skillet, drain excess fat. Add remaining ingredients, combine with beans in 3-quart (3 liter) casserole. Cover, bake at 275° (135°C) about 2 hours. Makes 6 to 8 servings.

[C] *Slow Cooker*

NEAPOLITAN LAYERS
Wonderful Italian flavor with American budget know-how

225 g	½ lb. ground beef
250 ml	1 cup finely chopped onion
	1 clove garlic, crushed
	2 (15-oz./425 g) cans Hunt's Tomato Herb Sauce
5 ml	1 teasp. seasoned salt
5 ml	1 teasp. oregano
	1 (10-oz./283 g) pkg. frozen chopped spinach, thawed
500 ml	1 pt. small curd cottage cheese
60 ml	¼ cup grated Parmesan cheese
	1 egg, beaten
.5 ml	⅛ teasp. pepper
225 g	8 ozs. elbow macaroni
225 g	½ lb. process American cheese, diced

Sauté ground beef, onion and garlic in 10-inch (25 cm) skillet. Add Hunt's Sauce, ½ *teaspoon* (3 ml) seasoned salt and oregano; simmer 5 minutes. Press spinach *very dry;* combine with cottage cheese, Parmesan cheese, egg, ½ *teaspoon* (3 ml) seasoned salt and pepper; set aside. Cook macaroni according to package directions. In 7½- x 12- x 1½-inch (18 x 30 x 4 cm) greased baking dish, layer *half each* of the macaroni, diced cheese and meat sauce. Cover with spinach mixture, then add remaining macaroni, diced cheese and meat sauce in layers. Bake at 375° (190°C) 35 to 40 minutes. Let stand a few minutes before serving. Makes 6 to 8 servings.

Use the baking utensil best suited to the recipe: 6- x 10- x 1½-inch or 1½-quart; 7½- x 12- x 1½-inch or 2-quart; 9- x 13- x 1½-inch or 3-quart.

Convenient One-Dish Meals

WUNDERSCHOEN EINTOPF C
Two ways to cook this tempting dish

900 g	2 lbs. pork shoulder, cut into 1-inch (3 cm) cubes
30 ml	2 Tablesp. pure vegetable oil
5 ml	1 teasp. salt
1 ml	¼ teasp. white pepper
	2 onions, chopped
15 ml	1 Tablesp. paprika
375 ml	1½ cups water
	1 (15-oz./425 g) can Hunt's Tomato Sauce with Tomato Bits
	2 cloves garlic, minced
	3 medium potatoes, cut into ½-inch (1 cm) thick slices
	1 (1-lb./453 g) can sauerkraut, drained
10 ml	2 to 3 teasp. caraway seed

Brown meat in oil in 12-inch (30 cm) skillet; sprinkle with salt and pepper. Add onion and paprika; cook until onion is soft. Drain fat. Add water, Hunt's Sauce and garlic; cover, simmer 25 minutes. Add remaining ingredients; mix well. Cover; simmer 1 hour longer. Makes 6 to 8 servings.

C *Slow Cooker*

Convenient One-Dish Meals

CHICKEN-CORN CHOWDER
A scrumptious Saturday night treat

675 g	1½ lbs. chicken wings, tips removed
125 ml	½ cup water
10 ml	2 teasp. salt
30 ml	2 Tablesp. chopped parsley
30 ml	2 Tablesp. chopped celery leaves
	2 carrots, diced
	2 medium potatoes, cubed
	2 ribs celery, sliced
	1 (15-oz./425 g) can Hunt's Tomato Sauce with Tomato Bits
	1 (1-lb. 1-oz./482 g) can cream-style corn
1 ml	¼ to ½ teasp. poultry seasoning

Place chicken wings in 2½-quart (2.5 liter) heavy saucepan with water, *1 teaspoon* (5 ml) salt, parsley and celery leaves; cover, simmer 15 minutes. Add carrots, potatoes, celery and *remaining 1 teaspoon* (5 ml) salt; simmer 15 to 20 minutes longer until chicken and vegetables are tender. Add Hunt's Sauce, corn and poultry seasoning; simmer, stirring, until heated through and slightly thickened. Makes 5 to 6 servings.

Convenient One-Dish Meals

ONE-PAN TACO CON QUESO

So easy, so good, it's a sure-fire favorite

225 g	½ lb. ground beef
	1 (15-oz./425 g) can Hunt's Tomato Sauce with Tomato Bits
	1 (15½-oz./439 g) can chili beans, undrained
	1 (3-oz./85 g) can French-fried onions
250 ml	1 cup coarsely crushed corn chips
250 ml	1 cup shredded process American cheese
500 ml	2 cups shredded lettuce
125 ml	½ cup sour cream

Cook ground beef in 10-inch (25 cm) skillet until it loses redness; drain fat. Set aside ¼ *cup (60 ml) tomato bits* from Hunt's Sauce for garnish; add *remainder* to ground beef along with chili beans and *half* of the French-fried onions; mix well. Simmer 10 minutes. Stir in *remainder* of French-fried onions and corn chips; sprinkle shredded cheese over all. Remove from heat. Arrange lettuce in layer over the cheese. Top with dollops of sour cream and garnish with reserved tomato bits. Makes 4 generous servings.

Convenient One-Dish Meals

SWISS STEAK, SUNDAY STYLE[C]

Baked potatoes and salad make an easy meal

675 g	1½ lbs. boneless round or chuck steak, 1 inch (3 cm) thick
30 ml	2 Tablesp. flour
8 ml	1½ teasp. salt
1 ml	¼ teasp. pepper
30 ml	2 Tablesp. pure vegetable oil
	1 onion, sliced
	1 clove garlic, minced
	1 (15-oz./425 g) can Hunt's Tomato Sauce with Tomato Bits
250 ml	1 cup water
250 ml	1 cup sliced celery
	3 carrots, sliced
250 ml	1 cup frozen peas, thawed

Cut steak into serving-size pieces. Combine flour, salt and pepper; pound into both sides of steak with mallet or edge of plate. Brown in oil in large skillet. Pour off excess fat. Add onion, garlic, Hunt's Sauce and water. Cover; simmer 1½ hours. Stir in celery and carrots; simmer 45 minutes longer. Sprinkle thawed peas over top last 15 minutes of cooking. Makes 4 to 5 servings.

C *Slow Cooker*

STOVE-TOP CHOPS AND BROWN RICE
Economical chops in a rich, flavorful sauce

800 g	1½ to 2 lbs.	pork shoulder chops or steaks
		Salt and pepper
30 ml	2 Tablesp.	pure vegetable oil
250 ml	1 cup	uncooked brown rice .
125 ml	½ cup *each:*	chopped onion and green pepper
125 ml	½ cup	sliced celery
500 ml	2 cups	water
	1 (8-oz./226 g) can	Hunt's Tomato Sauce
15 ml	1 Tablesp.	brown sugar, packed
250 ml	1 cup	frozen peas, thawed

Sprinkle chops with salt and pepper; brown in oil in 10-inch (25 cm) skillet. Remove chops. Add rice, onion, green pepper and celery to skillet drippings and sauté, stirring, until onion is soft. Add water, Hunt's Sauce, brown sugar and *1 teaspoon* (3 ml) salt; mix well. Bring to boil for 5 minutes. Return chops to skillet; cover; *simmer* 50 minutes. Sprinkle thawed peas over top. Turn off heat; cover and let stand 15 minutes. Makes 4 to 6 servings.

TRADITIONAL STEW POT^C
A magical one-dish marvel

675 g	1½ lbs.	lean stewing beef or bottom round, cut into 1-inch (3 cm) pieces
60 ml	¼ cup	flour
8 ml	1½ teasp.	salt
1 ml	¼ teasp.	pepper
30 ml	2 Tablesp.	pure vegetable oil
500 ml	2 cups	hot water
	1 (15-oz./425 g) can	Hunt's Tomato Sauce Special
	1 large	onion, quartered
3 ml	½ teasp.	basil
	2	potatoes, quartered
	3	carrots, sliced
	2 ribs	celery, chopped

Coat pieces of beef with mixture of flour, *1 teaspoon* (5 ml) salt and pepper, using it all. Brown in oil in heavy kettle or Dutch oven. Pour off excess fat. Add water, Hunt's Sauce, onions and basil. Cover; simmer 1½ hours. Add potatoes, carrots, celery and *remaining* ½ teaspoon (3 ml) salt. Cover and simmer ½ hour longer. Makes 4 to 6 servings. (See photo page 85)

^C*Slow Cooker*

HAM 'N' EGGS, HUNTER STYLE
Pretty party feast

450 g	1	lb. asparagus spears
125 ml	½	cup chopped onion
30 ml	2	Tablesp. butter or margarine
15 ml	1	Tablesp. flour
	1	(15-oz./425 g) can Hunt's Tomato Sauce Special
125 ml	½	cup dry white wine
60 ml	¼	cup water
3 ml	½	teasp. tarragon
	4	hard-cooked eggs
250 ml	1	cup diced cooked ham
	6	thin slices Italian bread, toasted and buttered
125 ml	½	cup shredded process American cheese

Cook and drain asparagus; keep warm.* In small skillet or saucepan, cook onion in butter until soft; blend in flour. Add Hunt's Sauce, wine, water and tarragon; cook, stirring, until smooth and blended. Slice *1* hard-cooked egg; set aside. Dice *remaining* hard-cooked eggs and add with ham to sauce. Arrange toast slices in individual oval-shaped ramekins or in one large shallow baking dish. Spoon *half* of ham and egg mixture equally over toast slices, top with equal "bundles" of asparagus spears. Spoon *remaining* ham and egg mixture over center of asparagus. Garnish with reserved slices of hard-cooked eggs; sprinkle with cheese. Bake· at 375° (190° C) 15 minutes. Makes 6 servings.

Or heat and drain 1 (1-lb./450 g) can asparagus spears.

Brown rice, like long or short grain white rice, triples in volume when cooked. Quick-cooking rice almost doubles when cooked.

ALL-IN-ONE
SPAGHETTI AND MEATBALLS
Easier than you ever dared dream

450 g	1	lb. lean ground beef
250 ml	1	cup fresh bread crumbs
125 ml	½	cup minced onion
5 ml	1	teasp. garlic salt
3 ml	½	teasp. oregano
	1	egg
	2	(15-oz./425 g) cans Hunt's Tomato Herb Sauce
225 g	8	ozs. spaghetti, cooked and drained
125 ml	½	cup water
30 ml	2	Tablesp. grated Parmesan cheese

Combine ground beef with next five ingredients and *½ cup* (125 ml) Hunt's Sauce; mix well. Form into 20 meatballs. Arrange in 9- x 13- x 1½-inch (23 x 33 x 4 cm) baking dish. Bake at 400° (205°C) 20 minutes. Remove from oven; drain fat. Arrange spaghetti around meatballs; pour *remaining* Hunt's Sauce mixed with water over all. Mix well. Sprinkle Parmesan over top. Bake 10 to 15 minutes longer until hot and bubbly. Makes 4 to 6 servings.

SAUCY SHORT RIB DINNER[C]
Fantastic cooked-in barbecue flavor

1700 g	3½	to 4 lbs. lean beef short ribs
		Salt and pepper
125 ml	½	cup chopped onion
30 ml	2	Tablesp. butter or margarine
	1	(8-oz./226 g) can Hunt's Tomato Sauce
85 ml	⅓	cup orange juice
85 ml	⅓	cup brown sugar, packed
15 ml	1	Tablesp. prepared mustard
5 ml	1	teasp. prepared horseradish
5 ml	1	teasp. seasoned salt
900 g	2	lbs. yellow winter squash, peeled

Arrange ribs in a 9- x 13- x 1½-inch (23 x 33 x 4 cm) baking dish. Sprinkle with salt and pepper. Cover; bake at 400° (205°C) 1½ hours. Meanwhile, sauté onion in butter in small saucepan until transparent. Add remaining ingredients, *except* squash; mix well. Simmer 10 minutes. Remove ribs from oven; drain fat. Cut squash in pieces and arrange between ribs; pour on *half* of sauce mixture. Lower temperature to 350° (175°C); bake, *uncovered,* 45 minutes to 1 hour longer. Turn ribs and squash once after ½ hour and pour on *remaining* sauce. Makes 6 servings.

[C]*Slow Cooker*

Convenient One-Dish Meals
MEXICALI BISCUIT BAKE
Attractive to serve, appetizing to eat

	1 (10-oz./283 g) can refrigerated biscuits
450 g	1 lb. ground beef
125 ml	½ cup *each:* chopped onion and green pepper
	1 (15½-oz./439 g) can chili beans, undrained
	1 (8-oz./226 g) can Hunt's Tomato Sauce
250 ml	1 cup shredded Cheddar cheese
125 ml	½ cup grated Parmesan cheese
5 ml	1 teasp. chili powder
3 ml	½ teasp. salt
125 ml	½ cup sliced pimiento-stuffed olives

Line sides of 10-inch (25 cm) pie pan with biscuits, pressing firmly into sides to form thin crust with tops of biscuits forming scalloped edge; set aside. In skillet, cook ground beef, onion and green pepper until beef loses redness; drain fat. Add chili beans, Hunt's Sauce, *half* the cheeses, chili powder and salt. Blend well. Spoon into biscuit lined pie pan. Arrange *remaining* cheeses over meat filling; top with olives. Bake at 375° (190°C) 20 minutes. Makes 4 to 6 servings.

Convenient One-Dish Meals
LASAGNA MARITIME
You'll love this budget lasagna variation

	1 (9½-oz./270 g) can tuna
	1 clove garlic, minced
125 ml	½ cup chopped onion
	1 (15-oz./425 g) can Hunt's Tomato Herb Sauce
125 ml	½ cup water
5 ml	1 teasp. salt
375 ml	1½ cups cottage cheese
	1 egg, beaten
60 ml	¼ cup grated Parmesan cheese
5 ml	1 teasp. leaf basil
225 g	8 ozs. lasagna noodles, cooked and drained
225 g	½ lb. mozzarella cheese, shredded

Drain *oil* from tuna into 10-inch (25 cm) skillet. Cook garlic and onion in tuna oil until onion is soft. Add Hunt's Sauce, water and salt. Simmer 10 minutes; then add tuna in chunks. Meanwhile, combine cottage cheese, egg, Parmesan cheese and basil. Arrange *half* of cooked noodles in bottom of 7½- x 12- x 1½-inch (18 x 30 x 4 cm) baking dish. Add layers of *half* of cottage cheese mixture, *half* of mozzarella and *half* of tuna and sauce. Repeat layers. Bake at 375° (190°C) 30 to 35 minutes. Let stand 10 minutes before serving. Makes 6 to 8 servings.

Convenient
One-Dish
Meals
CHICKEN JARDINIERE
Succulent chicken at its company best

	2 (2-lb./900 g) frying chickens, quartered
	1 clove garlic, minced
60 ml	¼ cup pure vegetable oil
5 ml	1 teasp. salt
.5 ml	⅛ teasp. pepper
	2 medium onions, thinly sliced
500 ml	2 cups chopped celery
	3 small carrots, cut into julienne strips
	1 (15-oz./425 g) can Hunt's Tomato Sauce Special
85 ml	⅓ cup white wine or water
1 ml	¼ teasp. ground marjoram

In skillet, brown chicken and garlic in oil; sprinkle with salt
and pepper. Arrange chicken in a 9- x 13- x 1½-inch (23 x
33 x 4 cm) baking dish. Lightly brown onions, celery and
carrots in skillet drippings; drain fat. Stir in remaining
ingredients. Simmer 10 minutes. Pour vegetable mixture over
chicken. Cover and bake at 350° (175°C) 40 to 50 minutes.
Makes 8 servings.

Convenient
One-Dish
Meals
BEEF CUBES SOMEWHAT STROGANOFF
Sour cream makes the delicious difference

450 g	1 lb. top round steak, ½ inch (1 cm) thick
45 ml	3 Tablesp. butter or margarine
5 ml	1 teasp. *each:* paprika and salt
	2 small onions, sliced
	1 (8-oz./226 g) can Hunt's Tomato Sauce with Mushrooms
125 ml	½ cup water
	1 can (about 2 oz./56 g) sliced mushrooms (optional)
125 ml	½ cup sour cream
	Hot buttered noodles
5 ml	1 teasp. dill weed

Cut steak into 1-inch (3 cm) pieces. Brown slowly in butter
in 10-inch (25 cm) skillet. Sprinkle with paprika and salt; add
onions and cook, stirring, until onions soften and separate
into rings. Stir in Hunt's Sauce, water and mushrooms. Cover;
simmer 1 to 1½ hours until meat is tender. Just before serving,
stir in sour cream. Serve over hot buttered noodles. Sprinkle
with dill weed. Makes 4 servings.

COUNTRY RIBS
AND CABBAGE DINNER^C

Wonderful country cooking aroma and flavor   97

1350 g	3	lbs. country-style pork ribs
60 ml	¼	cup pure vegetable oil
	1	(15-oz./425 g) can Hunt's Tomato Sauce with Tomato Bits
250 ml	1	cup water
30 ml	2	Tablesp. brown sugar, packed
15 ml	1	Tablesp. lemon juice
	1	chicken bouillon cube
5 ml	1	teasp. seasoned salt
.5 ml	⅛	teasp. pepper
	1	small head cabbage
	2	medium potatoes, cut into ½-inch-thick (1 cm) slices
3 ml	½	teasp. caraway seed (optional)

Brown ribs in oil in 12-inch (30 cm) skillet or Dutch oven; drain fat. Combine Hunt's Sauce with water, brown sugar, lemon juice, bouillon cube, salt and pepper in a small bowl; mix well. Pour all, *except ½ cup* (125 ml), over ribs. Bring to a boil; cover, simmer 50 to 60 minutes until almost tender. Turn pork ribs occasionally. Cut cabbage into 8 small wedges. Cover

Packaged bouillon cubes or granules are an inexpensive way to enhance the flavor of many casserole dishes, soups and stews.

with boiling water in a bowl; let stand 5 minutes and drain thoroughly. Place cabbage wedges and potato slices in sauce between ribs; sprinkle with caraway seed and *additional salt* and *pepper*. Pour *reserved sauce* mixture over all. Cover; simmer 25 to 30 minutes longer. Makes 4 to 6 servings.

^C*Slow Cooker*

Convenient One-Dish Meals
FISH AND CHIPS CASSEROLE
Frozen fish sticks all dressed up

	4 slices bacon, diced
250 ml	1 cup chopped onion
125 ml	½ cup chopped green pepper
	1 (15-oz./425 g) can Hunt's Tomato Sauce with Tomato Bits
	1 (12-oz./340 g) can whole kernel corn
8 ml	1½ teasp. salt
1 ml	¼ teasp. marjoram or thyme
	1 (14-oz./397 g) pkg. frozen fish sticks
250 ml	1 cup shredded Cheddar cheese
	1 (9-oz./255 g) pkg. frozen French fries

In skillet, cook bacon, onion and green pepper until almost tender. Stir in Hunt's Sauce, corn, *1 teaspoon* (5 ml) salt and marjoram. Arrange frozen fish sticks in bottom of lightly buttered 7½- x 12- x 1½-inch (18 x 30 x 4 cm) baking dish; sprinkle with *½ cup* (125 ml) cheese. Pour on tomato sauce mixture, then layer French fries over top and sprinkle with *remaining ½ teaspoon* (3 ml) salt. Bake at 375° (190°C) 35 minutes. Sprinkle *remaining* cheese over top; bake 10 minutes longer. Makes 4 to 6 servings.

Convenient One-Dish Meals
WESTERN DRUMSTICK BARBECUE
Sensational dinner for family and friends

1200 g	2 to 2½ lbs. frying chicken legs
	Salt and pepper
	1 (8-oz./226 g) can Hunt's Tomato Sauce
30 ml	2 Tablesp. molasses
15 ml	1 Tablesp. prepared mustard
.5 ml	⅛ teasp. liquid smoke
	1 (31-oz./879 g) can pork and beans
	1 (7-oz./198 g) can whole kernel corn
	1 pkg. (about 8-oz./226 g) corn muffin mix
30 ml	2 Tablesp. diced canned green chilies

Place chicken in 9- x 13- x 1½-inch (23 x 33 x 4 cm) baking dish; sprinkle with salt and pepper. Cover; bake at 425° (220°C) 30 minutes; drain excess fat. Meanwhile, combine Hunt's Sauce, molasses, mustard and liquid smoke. Use *half* to brush on "drumsticks"; arrange in center of dish. Spoon pork and beans mixed with corn on either side. Bake, *uncovered,* 15 minutes. Prepare muffin mix; fold in green chilies. Drop by spoonfuls over beans. Pour *remaining* sauce over chicken. Bake 15 to 20 minutes longer. Makes 4 to 6 servings.

PIZZA QUICHE

A French favorite with Italian seasonings

30 ml	2 Tablesp. flour
	3 eggs
250 ml	1 cup milk
	1 (8-oz./226 g) can Hunt's Tomato Sauce with Cheese
3 ml	½ teasp. salt
1 ml	¼ teasp. *each:* basil and oregano
	1 9-inch (23 cm) unbaked pie shell
170 ml	⅔ cup shredded Swiss cheese
	6 slices bacon, cooked and crumbled
15 ml	1 Tablesp. minced onion

Blend flour with eggs; beat in milk, ½ *cup* (125 ml) Hunt's Sauce, salt, basil and oregano. Bake pie shell at 400° (205°C) 5 minutes, remove; cover bottom with ⅓ *cup* (85 ml) cheese, sprinkle on bacon, onion and *remaining* cheese. Pour egg mixture carefully over all; continue to bake at 400° (205°C) 15 minutes. *Reduce heat to 325°* (165°C), bake 25 to 30 minutes longer until inserted silver knife comes out clean. Pour *remaining* Hunt's Sauce to form spokes atop filling. Let stand 10 minutes. Makes 4 to 6 servings.

PIGGY BANK PORK DINNER

An economical dish with an extra-tasty sauce

	1 (2-lb./900 g) boneless pork cottage roll
	Water
	12 small boiling onions
	6 whole cloves
	1 bay leaf
	6 yams, peeled and halved
45 ml	3 Tablesp. brown sugar, packed
10 ml	2 teasp. cornstarch
.5 ml	⅛ teasp. cinnamon
.5 ml	⅛ teasp. allspice
	1 (8-oz./226 g) can Hunt's Tomato Sauce
85 ml	⅓ cup seedless raisins

Place meat, 4 *cups* (1 liter) water, onions, cloves and bay leaf in Dutch oven. Cover, simmer 1 hour. Add yams; cover, simmer 25 minutes longer until tender. Meanwhile, combine brown sugar, cornstarch, cinnamon and allspice in a saucepan. Stir in Hunt's Sauce, ¼ *cup* (60 ml) water and raisins. Cook, stirring constantly until thick and shiny. Serve meat and vegetables with sauce. Makes 4 to 6 servings.

Food Odyssey to Foreign Lands

This is one of the most exciting
chapters of all, with recipes
that aren't necessarily difficult, but
ones that are definitely designed to
delight the palates of all who partake.
We've included some well-known
favorites, as well as some you've
probably never heard of before.

But try them all, because
once you do you'll discover that serving
dishes from foreign lands not only
makes entertaining more fun, but can
make you quite famous.

Opposite: Sukiyaki (page 105)

RATATOUILLE^M
A savory Mediterranean vegetable dish

	1 medium eggplant, peeled and cubed
	3 medium zucchini, cubed
	Salt
	1 green pepper, cut into medium squares
	1 clove garlic, crushed
	1 medium onion, thinly sliced
60 ml	¼ cup pure vegetable oil
	1 (15-oz./425 g) can Hunt's Tomato Sauce
	with Tomato Bits
3 ml	½ teasp. sugar
	Pepper
	Chopped parsley

Sprinkle eggplant and zucchini lightly with salt and let stand for 20 minutes. Blot excess moisture. Sauté with green pepper, garlic and onion in oil in 10-inch (25 cm) skillet for 10 minutes; stir gently. Add Hunt's Sauce and sugar, salt and pepper to taste. Cover, simmer 15 minutes until just tender; stir occasionally. Sprinkle with parsley. Makes 6 to 8 servings.

^M*Microwave*

INDONESIAN LAMB CURRY
Most impressive for a company dish

900 g	2 lbs. lamb shoulder, cubed
	1 onion, thinly sliced
	1 clove garlic, minced
45 ml	2 to 3 Tablesp. butter
	1 (8-oz./226 g) can Hunt's Tomato Sauce
125 ml	½ cup *each:* water and ketchup
30 ml	2 Tablesp. brown sugar, packed
10 ml	2 teasp. curry powder
5 ml	1 teasp. salt
	2 chicken bouillon cubes
	2 apples, pared, cored and sliced
	1 unpeeled orange, thinly sliced
125 ml	½ cup seedless raisins
1000 ml	4 cups hot cooked rice

Sauté lamb, onion and garlic in butter in a large skillet or Dutch oven, until onion is soft and lamb loses redness. Stir in remaining ingredients, *except* rice; blend well. Simmer, covered, 1 hour over medium heat; stir occasionally. Serve over hot cooked rice. Makes 6 to 8 servings.

Opposite: Indonesian Lamb Curry

KALDOLMAR

SWEDISH CABBAGE ROLLS
A traditional dish prepared in the traditional way

	1	large head Savoy or green cabbage
		Boiling water
225 g	½	lb. *each:* ground lean pork and veal or
		1 lb. (450 g) lean ground beef
125 ml	½	cup cooked rice
	1	egg
60 ml	¼	cup minced onion
15 ml	1	Tablesp. minced parsley
3 ml	½	teasp. salt
1 ml	¼	teasp. pepper
30 ml	2 to 3	Tablesp. pure vegetable oil
	1	(15-oz./425 g) can Hunt's Tomato Sauce
250 ml	1	cup beef bouillon
1 ml	¼	teasp. dill weed
60 ml	¼	cup water
30 ml	2	Tablesp. flour
60 ml	¼	cup sour cream

Core cabbage and cover with boiling water; let stand 5 minutes or until leaves are limp enough to separate easily. Combine pork, veal, rice, egg, onion, parsley, salt and pepper; mix gently but thoroughly. Place 2 to 3 tablespoons (30 to 45 ml) meat mixture in center of each leaf. Fold the sides of the leaf over meat mixture; roll up; secure with toothpicks. Brown quickly in oil in 12-inch (30 cm) skillet. Drain excess fat. Combine Hunt's Sauce, bouillon and dill weed. Pour over cabbage rolls. Bring to a boil. Cover; simmer 40 minutes. Place cabbage rolls on warm serving platter. Combine water and flour and use to thicken skillet juices. Stir in sour cream. Serve over cabbage rolls. Makes 6 servings.

Proportion your own "meat loaf mix" by allowing ⅔ ground beef to ⅓ unseasoned ground pork.

SZEKELY GULYAS
HUNGARIAN PORK GOULASH
The flavor speaks for itself

1350 g	3 lbs. pork shoulder, cut into 1-inch (3 cm) cubes
60 ml	¼ cup pure vegetable oil
	3 large onions, chopped
	2 green peppers, cut into strips
15 ml	1 Tablesp. Hungarian paprika
5 ml	1 teasp. crushed dill seed
15 ml	1 Tablesp. brown sugar, packed
125 ml	½ cup water
	1 (15-oz./425 g) can Hunt's Tomato Sauce
	1 (27-oz./765 g) can sauerkraut
3 ml	½ teasp. salt
.5 ml	⅛ teasp. pepper
250 ml	1 cup sour cream

Brown cubed pork in oil in Dutch oven. Stir in onions, green pepper strips and paprika; cook until onions are soft. Stir in remaining ingredients, *except* sour cream. Bring to a boil. Cover; simmer 40 minutes. Top with sour cream. Makes 6 to 8 servings.

SUKIYAKI
JAPANESE BEEF AND VEGETABLES
Especially good with rice and hot sake

225 g	½ lb. beef tenderloin, sliced paper thin
	1 onion, thinly sliced
60 ml	¼ cup sliced mushrooms
	1 carrot, thinly sliced diagonally
	1 rib celery, sliced diagonally
	1 bunch fresh spinach, washed and trimmed
	1 cup bean threads or cellophane noodles
	1 (8-oz./226 g) can Hunt's Tomato Sauce
85 ml	⅓ cup soy sauce
60 ml	¼ cup sake or sherry
60 ml	¼ cup sugar

On a large platter, arrange mounds of beef, onions, mushrooms, carrots, celery, spinach and bean threads. Combine remaining ingredients in a small bowl; blend well. Heat a large electric skillet or wok over high heat. Add *half* the meat; sear until beef loses its redness. Place *half of each* vegetable in skillet; stir-fry. Pour *half* the sauce mixture over all. Simmer 5 minutes, stirring often. Serve at once. Repeat process for second serving. Makes 2 servings. (See photo page 101)

BOEUF BOURGUIGNONNE^C

Food Odyssey to Foreign Lands

BEEF BURGUNDY
A classic French dish that's truly gourmet

60 ml	¼ cup diced salt pork
60 ml	¼ cup melted butter
	12 small pearl or boiling onions
115 g	¼ lb. fresh mushrooms, sliced
	2 shallots, sliced (optional)
	3 to 4 carrots, sliced
	1 clove garlic, minced
800 g	1½ to 2 lbs. top round of beef
30 ml	2 Tablesp. flour
5 ml	1 teasp. salt
1 ml	¼ teasp. coarse ground pepper
250 ml	1 cup beef bouillon
	1 (15-oz./425 g) can Hunt's Tomato Sauce
375 ml	1½ cups red burgundy wine
	1 bay leaf
3 ml	½ teasp. bouquet garni seasonings
	3 sprigs parsley

Cook salt pork in boiling water to cover 5 minutes; drain. Cook in butter in Dutch oven until golden. Remove pork; set aside. Add onions, mushrooms, shallots, carrots and garlic and sauté in drippings. Trim fat from beef; cut into bite-size pieces. Add to vegetables; brown quickly. Stir in flour, salt and pepper; cook until bubbly. Stir in reserved salt pork and remaining ingredients; bring to a boil. Cover; simmer 40 minutes, stirring once or twice. Remove bay leaf and parsley before serving. Makes 6 to 8 servings.

Keep meals interesting. Try an entirely new and different main dish recipe at least once a week.

^C*Slow Cooker*

KARABAKH
STRING BEANS IN A SPECIAL SAUCE
Uniquely cooked and sauced, uniquely Russian

	2 cups thinly sliced onions
450 g	1 lb. fresh string beans, trimmed
60 ml	¼ cup butter
	1 (15-oz./425 g) can Hunt's Tomato Sauce Special
1000 ml	1 qt. water
5 ml	1 teasp. *each:* salt and leaf basil, crumbled
250 ml	1 cup sour cream
	1 egg
3 ml	½ teasp. salt
1 ml	¼ teasp. coarse ground pepper

In a Dutch oven, sauté onion and string beans in butter until onions are soft and beans bright green. Stir in next four ingredients. Simmer, uncovered, over medium heat 45 minutes or until vegetables are tender and most of the liquid has evaporated; stir occasionally. Meanwhile, in a medium bowl, combine sour cream, egg and seasonings; blend well. Stir into beans. Serve at once. Makes 4 to 6 servings.

STEAK AND KIDNEY PIE
A jolly-well delicious dish from the British Isles

900 g	2 lbs. round steak, cut into 1-inch (3 cm) cubes
225 g	½ lb. beef kidneys, cut into 1-inch (3 cm) cubes
170 ml	⅔ cup flour
8 ml	1½ teasp. salt
3 ml	½ teasp. nutmeg
1 ml	¼ teasp. pepper
45 ml	3 Tablesp. pure vegetable oil
125 ml	½ cup finely chopped onion
60 ml	¼ cup chopped fresh parsley
	1 (8-oz./226 g) can Hunt's Tomato Sauce with Mushrooms
	Pastry for 2-crust 9-inch (23 cm) pie

Coat steak and kidney cubes with mixture of flour, salt, nutmeg and pepper, using it all. Brown in oil in 12-inch (30 cm) skillet; add onion, sauté lightly. Stir in parsley and Hunt's Sauce. Cover; simmer 10 to 15 minutes over low heat. Stir often. Meanwhile, fit *half* of pastry into bottom of 9-inch (23 cm) pie pan. Fill with hot meat mixture. Top with remaining pastry. Seal edges; flute. Make several slits in top of pastry to vent. Bake at 325° (165°C) 1½ hours. Makes 6 to 8 servings.

SAUERBRATEN^C

Make sure to plan ahead when you make this German favorite

250 ml	1	cup water
125 ml	½	cup dry red wine
125 ml	½	cup wine vinegar
	1	onion, thinly sliced
	8	cloves
	5	peppercorns
	2	bay leaves
	1	cinnamon stick
	1	(4-lb./1800 g) boneless beef pot roast
45 ml	3	Tablesp. pure vegetable oil
125 ml	½	cup finely chopped onion
125 ml	½	cup finely chopped carrots
60 ml	¼	cup finely chopped celery
	1	(8-oz./226 g) can Hunt's Tomato Sauce with Mushrooms
30 ml	2	Tablesp. sugar
125 ml	½	cup finely crushed gingersnaps
30 ml	2	Tablesp. flour

Combine first 8 ingredients in a large glass bowl; blend well. Place roast in marinade; cover tightly. Marinate in refrigerator 2 to 3 days. Turn at least twice a day. To cook, drain meat well. Strain and *reserve 2½ cups* (625 ml) marinade. Brown meat on all sides in oil in large kettle or Dutch oven; remove. Sauté onions, carrots and celery in drippings until onions are tender. Add *reserved* marinade, Hunt's Sauce and sugar; blend well. Return browned roast to mixture; cover, simmer 3 to 4 hours over medium heat. Stir in gingersnaps mixed with flour last 30 minutes of cooking time. Makes 6 to 8 servings.

It's seldom that cost per pound makes a cut of meat costly. Figure the cost per serving.

^C*Slow Cooker*

GERSTENSUPPE

Stick-to-the-ribs barley soup from Switzerland

	1 (15-oz./425 g) can Hunt's Tomato Sauce
2.5 l	2½ quarts water
450 g	1 lb. smoked ham hocks
125 ml	½ cup pearl barley
5 ml	1 teasp. salt
	3 or 4 peppercorns or ¼ teasp. black pepper
250 ml	1 cup chopped leeks
125 ml	½ cup sliced celery
125 ml	½ cup thinly sliced onion
	1 large potato, pared and cubed
250 ml	1 cup heavy cream or evaporated milk
15 ml	1 Tablesp. cornstarch

In a heavy kettle or Dutch oven, combine first six ingredients. Heat to boiling; simmer, covered, 45 minutes. Add leeks, celery, onion and potatoes; simmer 30 minutes longer or until vegetables are tender. Remove ham hock; cut meat from bone and return to soup. Combine cream and cornstarch in small bowl; stir into soup mixture; simmer 2 minutes. Makes 6 to 8 servings.

HERBED LEG OF LAMB

Two favorite Greek foods make an elegant dish

	1 (4½- to 5-lb./2100 g) leg of lamb
	3 cloves garlic, slivered
15 ml	1 Tablesp. lemon juice
10 ml	2 teasp. salt
5 ml	1 teasp. oregano
3 ml	½ teasp. *each:* pepper, powdered thyme, marjoram and dry mustard
	4 small artichokes
	1 unpeeled lemon, thinly sliced
	1 (15-oz./425 g) can Hunt's Tomato Herb Sauce
500 ml	2 cups water

Make several slits in leg of lamb with tip of knife; insert a sliver of garlic into each. Make a paste of lemon juice, salt, oregano, pepper, thyme, marjoram and dry mustard; spread over entire surface of lamb. Place on rack in large shallow baking pan. Roast at 375° (190°C) 1 hour, basting occasionally with drippings. Meanwhile, trim artichoke stems, snip off tips, cut in half. Remove lamb from oven; remove rack and drain excess fat; return lamb to baking pan. Arrange artichoke halves, cut side down, and lemon slices around lamb. Combine Hunt's Sauce and water. Pour over artichokes. Bake 1 to 1½ hours longer, basting occasionally. Makes 6 to 8 servings.

MOUSSAKA

This dish makes eggplant famous

450 g	1 lb. ground lamb or beef
125 ml	½ cup finely chopped onion
30 ml	2 Tablesp. minced parsley
3 ml	½ teasp. salt
.5 ml	⅛ teasp. *each:* nutmeg and pepper
	1 small eggplant (about 1 lb./450 g)
85 ml	⅓ cup fine dry bread crumbs
85 ml	⅓ cup grated Parmesan cheese
	1 egg, slightly beaten
85 ml	⅓ cup pure vegetable oil
	1 (15-oz./425 g) can Hunt's Tomato Sauce
60 ml	¼ cup dry red wine
1 ml	¼ teasp. sugar

Cook lamb, onion, parsley, salt, nutmeg and pepper in skillet until onion is soft; drain fat. Cut eggplant into ¾-inch (2 cm) slices. Combine bread crumbs and *2 tablespoons* (30 ml) Parmesan; mix well. Dip eggplant slices into egg, then coat with crumb mixture. Brown in oil in 12-inch (30 cm) skillet. Top with meat mixture. Combine Hunt's Sauce, wine and sugar; pour over all. Sprinkle with *remaining* Parmesan. Cover; simmer 40 minutes. Makes 4 to 6 servings.

ARROZ CON POLLO

Spanish seasoned one-pan favorite

1200 g	2½ to 3 lbs. frying chicken pieces
60 ml	¼ cup pure vegetable oil
	Salt and pepper
	2 medium onions, thinly sliced
	1 large green pepper, chopped
	1 clove garlic, minced
500 ml	2 cups uncooked rice
	1 (8-oz./226 g) can Hunt's Tomato Sauce
	3 (10¾-oz./305 g) cans chicken broth
3 ml	½ teasp. ground cumin
1 ml	¼ teasp. powdered saffron
	Sliced pimiento
	Ripe olives

Brown chicken pieces in oil in 12-inch (30 cm) skillet until golden. Sprinkle with salt and pepper. Remove from skillet. Cook and stir onions, green pepper, garlic and rice in skillet until oil is absorbed. Stir in Hunt's Sauce, chicken broth, cumin and saffron. Arrange chicken pieces over rice. Bring to a boil. Cover; simmer 40 minutes. Garnish with sliced pimiento and olives before serving. Makes 8 servings.

UKRAINIAN BORSCHT^C

800 g	1½ to 2 lbs. top round of beef
30 ml	2 Tablesp. pure vegetable oil
1250 ml	5 cups hot water
	3 beef bouillon cubes
	1 bay leaf
8 ml	1½ teasp. salt
	1 soup bone
	1 (15-oz./425 g) can Hunt's Tomato Sauce with Tomato Bits
	1 bunch (about 5 medium) beets, pared and cut into narrow strips
500 ml	2 cups chopped cabbage
375 ml	1½ cups thinly sliced carrots
250 ml	1 cup sliced celery
250 ml	1 cup chopped onion
	Sour cream

Trim all fat from beef; cut into bite-size pieces; brown in oil in Dutch oven. Add water, bouillon cubes, bay leaf, salt and soup bone; bring to a full boil; skim excess fat. Stir in Hunt's Sauce and vegetables; bring to a full boil. Cover; simmer 40 minutes, stirring once or twice. Serve in large soup bowls topped with dollop of sour cream. Makes 6 to 8 servings (about 3 quarts/3 liters).

Many recipes in this book are suited to slow cooker preparation, by adapting temperature and cooking time.

^C*Slow Cooker*

Simple Dishes made Elegant

Elegance can be easy when you
take an everyday simple dish and brighten
it up with new taste appeal and some
nifty serving ideas.

In this chapter, we've included
five complete menus, along with fun
ways to dress up your table, as
well as some of our favorite
recipes. You'll find every one
easy to make, elegant to serve,
and economical, too.

It's the last-minute find of the year. Our just-developed 10-minute spaghetti sauce, with the real flavor that used to take hours.

The "Elegant" Table

A warm Italian glow of red, white and green. Checked table cloth. Red napkins. Candles in old wine bottles. Stack assorted dry pastas (ribbons, fettuccini, curly macaroni shapes) in glass jars for a centerpiece.

10-Minute Spaghetti and Meat Sauce
Bread Sticks
Anti-Work Antipasto Salad
Spumoni Ice Cream

Simple Dishes made Elegant

10-MINUTE SPAGHETTI AND MEAT SAUCE

225 g	½ lb. ground beef
	1 (15-oz./425 g) can Hunt's Tomato Herb Sauce
250 ml	1 cup beer, water or mixture of both
30 ml	2 Tablesp. grated Parmesan cheese
15 ml	1 Tablesp. instant minced onion
5 ml	1 teasp. oregano
3 ml	½ teasp. garlic powder
3 ml	½ teasp. sugar
3 ml	½ teasp. salt
	1 beef bouillon cube
225 g	8 ozs. spaghetti, cooked and drained

Brown ground beef in 10-inch (25 cm) skillet, drain. Add remaining ingredients, *except* spaghetti. Bring to a boil; simmer 5 minutes, stirring occasionally. Serve over hot cooked spaghetti. Makes 4 servings.

ANTI-WORK ANTIPASTO SALAD

Combine *2 cups* (500 ml) torn lettuce with *½ cup* (125 ml) *each:* sliced fresh mushrooms, sliced pepperoni or salami, sliced stuffed olives, sliced green onions and sliced radishes. At serving time, toss with Italian dressing. Makes 4 servings.

A CAMPFIRE DINNER WITHOUT LEAVING HOME

Here are all the good smells and flavor of a hearty beef and bean chuckwagon dinner. Piping hot biscuits and a relish plate keep it simple. With a special dessert, you'll welcome unexpected guests for this one.

The "Elegant" Table

Chuckwagon Dinner served in a heavy black iron kettle can be the centerpiece feature. Use tin plates and cups from your camping supplies. Add a few country touches . . . silverware wrapped in bandana napkins and placemats cut from colorful checked oilcloth.

*Chuckwagon
Beef and Beans
Baking Powder
Biscuits
Roundup Relishes
Cowhand Sundae*

*Simple
Dishes
a made
Elegant*

CHUCKWAGON BEEF AND BEANS

675 g	1½	lbs. boneless chuck steak, cut into bite-size pieces
30 ml	2	Tablesp. pure vegetable oil
	1	(15½-oz./439 g) can small red beans, drained
	1	(15-oz./439 g) can pinto beans, drained
	1	(15-oz./425 g) can Hunt's Tomato Sauce
60 ml	¼	cup dark corn syrup
60 ml	¼	cup vinegar
30 ml	2	Tablesp. instant minced onion
5 ml	1	teasp. barbecue spice

In 12-inch (30 cm) skillet, brown steak pieces in oil. Add remaining ingredients. Blend well. Simmer 30 minutes or until beef is tender. Makes 4 to 5 servings.

ROUNDUP RELISHES

Select crisp young garden vegetables. Include zucchini slices, carrot, celery and cucumber sticks, cauliflowerets, green pepper rings and green onions.

COWHAND SUNDAES

Toast frozen waffles, top with a favorite flavor ice cream and serve with help-yourself sundae sauces and nuts.

Opposite: Chuckwagon Beef and Beans

CHICKEN WAIKIKI
Serve right in pineapple shells for a party touch

	1 small fresh pineapple
1200 g	2½ to 3 lbs. frying chicken pieces
45 ml	3 Tablesp. pure vegetable oil
	1 (8-oz./226 g) can Hunt's Tomato Sauce
60 ml	¼ cup cider vinegar
60 ml	¼ cup light corn syrup
3 ml	½ teasp. salt
.5 ml	⅛ teasp. pepper
60 ml	¼ cup light brown sugar, packed
15 ml	1 Tablesp. cornstarch
625 ml	2½ cups hot cooked rice

Cut pineapple in half lengthwise. Carefully remove pineapple fruit from shells, leaving walls about ⅜ inch (1 cm) thick. Set shells aside. Cut pineapple into bite-size chunks. Pour off pineapple juice that accumulates in shell, *reserving ¼ cup (60 ml) juice.* In 12-inch (30 cm) skillet, brown chicken in oil; drain fat. While chicken browns, combine *reserved* pineapple juice with Hunt's Sauce, vinegar, corn syrup, salt and pepper in saucepan. Stir in brown sugar mixed with cornstarch. Simmer until clear and thickened, stirring constantly. Add pineapple chunks to chicken in skillet. Pour sauce over all. Cover, simmer 15 minutes. To serve, arrange in reserved pineapple shells. Serve with hot cooked rice. Makes 4 servings.

If desired, 1 (20-oz./567 g) can of pineapple chunks, drained, and ¼ cup (60 ml) reserved pineapple syrup can be substituted for the fresh pineapple.

Opposite: Chicken Waikiki

FREEZER-TO-OVEN ROAST
An extra-juicy treat

1700 g	3½- to 4-pound frozen rump roast, diamond or watermelon cut
	Salt and pepper
	1 (15-oz./425 g) can Hunt's Tomato Herb Sauce
60 ml	¼ cup red wine or water
30 ml	2 Tablesp. grated Parmesan cheese

Sprinkle frozen roast generously on all sides with salt and pepper. Place in center of large piece of heavy duty aluminum foil. Seal top and ends, using drugstore fold. Place in 9- x 13- x 2-inch (23 x 33 x 5 cm) baking pan. Roast at 400° (205°C) 2½ hours. Open foil carefully at one end to allow excess steam to escape; then open foil away from roast completely; skim excess fat, if necessary. Pour *1 cup* (250 ml) Hunt's Sauce over and around roast. Reseal foil; lower oven temperature to 350° (175°C), roast 45 minutes longer. Open foil away from roast; pour *remaining* Hunt's Sauce mixed with wine over all; sprinkle with Parmesan cheese. Return to oven 5 to 10 minutes. Makes 6 servings, with some roast left over.

DRESS-IT-UP CHILI[M]
A do-it-yourself dish everyone loves

335 g	¾ lb. ground beef
	2 (15½-oz./439 g) cans kidney beans, drained
	1 (14½-oz./425 g) can whole tomatoes
	2 (8-oz./226 g) cans Hunt's Tomato Sauce with Cheese
60 ml	¼ cup instant minced onion
10 ml	2 teasp. chili powder
5 ml	1 teasp. salt
5 ml	1 teasp. ground cumin
	Dress-up Toppings*

Brown ground beef in Dutch oven; drain fat. Add remaining ingredients, *except* toppings; mix well. Cover and simmer 20 minutes. Prepare small bowls of Dress-up Toppings. Let each person add the toppings of his choice. Makes 4 (1½-cup/375 ml) servings.

*Dress-up Toppings: Sliced green onions, sour cream, cheese, avocado slices, crumbled bacon, crushed corn chips.

M*Microwave*

MEAT LOAF TURNS OVER A NEW LEAF

Fast-baking little meat loaves, one per person, topped with potato crowns. Plus a quick trick with green beans . . . and more for a savory meal.

The "Elegant" Table

Think of fall leaf colors. Use gold place mats. Put a real fall leaf on each napkin, and a candle into a cored apple at each place.

Double-Deck
Beef and Potatoes
Glazed Peach Halves
Green Beans Royale
Brown 'n Serve Bread
Autumn Apple
and Cheese Wedges

DOUBLE-DECK BEEF AND POTATOES

675 g	1½	lbs. ground beef and pork for meat loaf
	1	(8-oz./226 g) can Hunt's Tomato Sauce with Mushrooms
	2	slices bread, crumbled
	1	egg
60 ml	¼	cup chopped green pepper
30 ml	2	Tablesp. instant chopped onion
8 ml	1½	teasp. salt
1 ml	¼	teasp. pepper
750 ml	3	cups hot mashed potatoes
		Paprika

In medium bowl, combine all ingredients, *except* potatoes and paprika; mix thoroughly. Shape into 6 individual loaves; place in shallow baking pan. Bake at 450° (230°C) 20 minutes. Top each loaf with ½ cup (125 ml) dollop of potatoes. Bake 10 minutes longer. Sprinkle with paprika. Makes 6 servings.

GLAZED PEACH HALVES

Combine *6 tablespoons* (90 ml) ketchup, *2 tablespoons* (30 ml) brown sugar and *½ teaspoon* (3 ml) grated orange peel. Spoon into centers of *6* canned peach halves. Bake with meat loaves last 10 minutes. Makes 6 servings.

GREEN BEANS ROYALE

In a saucepan, combine *2 (10-oz./283 g) pkgs.* frozen French-style green beans, *1 cup* (250 ml) water, 3 chicken bouillon cubes and *1 teaspoon* (5 ml) nutmeg. Cook according to directions on green bean package. Makes 6 servings.

Simple Dishes made Elegant

FLIP-FLOP CHEESEBURGER PIE
A giant cheeseburger with its own special bun

675 g	1½	lbs. ground beef
	4	green onions, chopped
	1	(15-oz./425 g) can Hunt's Tomato Sauce Special
375 ml	1½	cups shredded process American cheese
5 ml	1	teasp. prepared mustard
3 ml	½	teasp. salt
1 ml	¼	teasp. pepper
375 ml	1½	cups all-purpose baking mix
90 ml	¼	cup *plus* 2 Tablesp. cold water

In 10-inch (25 cm) ovenproof skillet, brown beef with onions; drain fat. Stir in Hunt's Sauce, *1 cup* (250 ml) cheese, mustard, salt and pepper. Simmer, uncovered, 10 minutes. Meanwhile, stir together baking mix and water. Shape dough into ball on floured board; knead 5 times; press into 9½-inch (24 cm) circle. Arrange meat mixture evenly over bottom of skillet. Carefully place dough on top of meat. Bake at 450° (230°C) 10 to 12 minutes. Let stand a few minutes. Invert onto serving platter. Sprinkle with *remaining* ½ cup (125 ml) cheese. Cut into wedges. Makes 6 servings.

Simple Dishes made Elegant

PORK CHOPS AND RICE PARMIGIANA
A flavorful combination in a hearty sauce

	6	loin pork chops, ½ inch (1 cm) thick
15 ml	1	Tablesp. pure vegetable oil
		Salt and pepper
	1	(15-oz./425 g) can Hunt's Tomato Herb Sauce
375 ml	1½	cups water
180 ml	¾	cup uncooked rice
60 ml	¼	cup chopped green pepper
	6	thin slices mozzarella cheese
30 ml	2	Tablesp. grated Parmesan cheese

Brown chops in oil in 12-inch (30 cm) skillet. Sprinkle with salt and pepper. Remove chops and set aside; drain excess fat. Add *1½ cups* (375 ml) Hunt's Sauce, water, rice, green pepper and *½ teaspoon* (3 ml) salt to skillet. Bring to a boil, return chops to skillet; cover. Simmer 25 to 30 minutes. Last 10 minutes, top chops with mozzarella slices and *remaining* Hunt's Sauce; sprinkle Parmesan over all. Makes 4 to 6 servings.

BEFORE YOU CAN SAY BOO! STEW IN A PUMPKIN

Try our leftover beef recipe . . . and
suddenly, beef stew is new!
And a lot quicker to make.

The "Elegant" Table

The Great Pumpkin Patch at your
table, and a couple of orange
candles, will do the trick for
this treat. Around your Stew in
a Pumpkin, a few Halloween
cutouts would be fun, and fall
harvest things like squash in
pretty shapes, cranberries, green apples.

*Stew in a Pumpkin
Trick or Treat Salad
Double Bubble Bread
Hot Apple Pie*

*Simple
Dishes
made
Elegant* ## STEW IN A PUMPKIN

125 ml	½	cup *each:* chopped onion, celery and mushrooms
30 ml	2	Tablesp. pure vegetable oil
500 ml	2	cups 1-inch (3 cm) cubes cooked beef
	1	(15-oz./425 g) can Hunt's Tomato Sauce with Tomato Bits
30 ml	2	Tablesp. chopped parsley
	1	(16-oz./450 g) can *each:* drained sliced carrots and whole potatoes, cubed
15 ml	1	Tablesp. Worcestershire
5 ml	1	teasp. salt
	1	(¾-oz./20 g) pkg. brown gravy mix, blended with ¾ cup (180 ml) water
	1	medium pumpkin

In a heavy kettle, cook onion, celery and mushrooms in oil
until tender. Add remaining ingredients, *except* pumpkin, and
blend well. Simmer 10 minutes. Meanwhile, hollow out and
rinse pumpkin; heat at 400° (205°C) 10 minutes. Fill pumpkin
with hot stew. Makes 4 servings.

TRICK OR TREAT SALAD

Combine grapefruit sections, orange sections and seeded Tokay
grapes to make 3 cups (750 ml). Toss with your favorite fruit
salad dressing. Makes 4 servings.

DOUBLE-BUBBLE BREAD

Cut *2 cans* refrigerated biscuits into quarters and dip in ½ *cup*
(125 ml) melted butter. Layer "bubbles" and ½ *cup* (125 ml)
grated Parmesan cheese in a 5- to 6-cup (1.5 liter) ring mold.
Drizzle remaining butter over top; bake at 400° 20 minutes.

TANGY MEATBALL KABOBS
Just add noodles or rice for a special meal

565 g	1¼ lbs. lean ground beef
	1 egg, slightly beaten
60 ml	¼ cup fine dry bread crumbs
3 ml	½ teasp. *each:* garlic salt, salt and pepper
	6 10-inch (25 cm) skewers
	1 small green pepper, cut into 1-inch (3 cm) squares
	1 (16-oz./450 g) can whole onions, drained
	1 (16-oz./450 g) can whole baby carrots, drained
	2 (8-oz./226 g) cans Hunt's Tomato Sauce with Onions
125 ml	½ cup water
30 ml	2 Tablesp. Worcestershire
30 ml	2 Tablesp. brown sugar
8 ml	1½ teasp. dry mustard

Combine ground beef, egg, bread crumbs, garlic salt, salt and pepper; mix well. Shape into 18 meatballs. In 9- x 13- x 2-inch (23 x 33 x 5 cm) baking pan, bake meatballs at 400° (205°C) for 15 minutes. Drain fat. On each skewer, alternate 3 meatballs with green pepper, onions and carrots. Place kabobs in baking pan. Combine remaining ingredients. Pour over kabobs. Bake 20 minutes longer, basting frequently with sauce. Serve kabobs and sauce on hot cooked rice or noodles, if desired. Makes 6 servings.

ROSY GLAZED HAM AND YAMS^M
Add a festive look; stud the ham with whole cloves

	1 ham steak, 1½ inches (4 cm) thick
	1 (1-lb. 13-oz./900 g) can whole yams, drained
	1 (8-oz./226 g) can Hunt's Tomato Sauce
180 ml	¾ cup orange marmalade
10 ml	2 teasp. prepared mustard
10 ml	2 teasp. vinegar
1 ml	¼ teasp. ground cloves
.5 ml	⅛ teasp. cinnamon

Place ham and yams in 7½- x 12- x 1½-inch (18 x 30 x 4 cm) baking dish. Combine remaining ingredients with rotary beater; pour over ham and yams. Bake at 350° (175°C) for 30 minutes. Makes 4 to 5 servings.

^M*Microwave*

Saucy Creole fish and rice, served with Spinach Spoon Bread. For a dessert—a very fresh idea. Ice cream in dixie paper cups, topped with chocolate cookie crumbs. Each cup goes in a tiny clay flower pot (a new one). Put paper flowers into ice cream . . . for a flower pot dessert!

The "Elegant" Table

Pick up green paper mats, green napkins, and a fresh, green potted plant from your market (or use your own). "Plant" two green candles in the dirt and use as a fresh centerpiece.

*Simple
Seafood Creole
Rice
Lemon Wedges
Spinach Spoon Bread
Ice Cream Flower Pots*

Simple Dishes made Elegant

SIMPLE SEAFOOD CREOLE[M]

	½ green pepper, chopped
	1 clove garlic, minced
10 ml	2 teasp. pure vegetable oil
	1 (15-oz./425 g) can Hunt's Tomato Sauce Special
5 ml	1 teasp. salt
	1 bay leaf
1 ml	¼ teasp. thyme
.5 ml	⅛ teasp. pepper
	1 (6-oz./170 g) pkg. frozen crab, thawed
450 g	1 lb. fresh or frozen halibut or whitefish, cut into bite-size pieces
750 ml	3 cups hot cooked rice

In a 10-inch (25 cm) skillet, sauté green pepper and garlic in oil until tender. Add Hunt's Sauce, salt, bay leaf, thyme and pepper. Simmer 5 minutes, stirring occasionally. Add seafood; simmer 5 minutes longer. Remove bay leaf. Serve over hot cooked rice. Makes 4 servings.

M*Microwave*

SPINACH SPOON BREAD
Combine *1 (8-oz./225 g) pkg.* corn muffin mix, *½ cup* (125 ml) shredded sharp Cheddar cheese, *2 tablespoons* (30 ml) crumbled cooked bacon and *½ teaspoon* (3 ml) seasoned salt. Add *2 egg yolks* and *½ cup* (125 ml) water; blend thoroughly. Fold in *2 egg whites*, beaten stiff, and *1 (10-oz./283 g) pkg.* frozen chopped spinach, thawed and pressed dry. Bake in a greased 8-inch (20 cm) square pan at 400° (205°C) 20 to 25 minutes. Serve with a generous pat of butter. Makes 8 servings.

Delicious Low·cost Dishes

Winning the battle of the food
budget can be an absolutely delicious
experience, especially with the recipes
you'll find in this chapter.

We've included meatless dishes so
nutritious and full of robust flavor, no
one will miss the meat at all. And
then in other recipes, we've shown
you how to stretch a little meat a long,
long way by using it in combination with
other low-cost, high-protein foods.

Opposite: Deviled Eggs en Casserole (page 129)

Delicious Low-cost Dishes FABULOUS OXTAIL STEW

French provincial. . . Delicious and economical

900 g	2 lbs. oxtail slices*
1000 ml	1 qt. boiling water
10 ml	2 teasp. chicken broth granules
10 ml	2 teasp. salt
5 ml	1 teasp. fines herbes or bouquet garni
.5 ml	⅛ teasp. pepper
	1 (15-oz./425 g) can Hunt's Tomato Sauce Special
	1 medium onion, sliced
375 ml	1½ cups *each:* 1-inch (3 cm) slices of carrots, celery and parsnips
115 g	¼ lb. green beans

Brown oxtail slices lightly in heated deep heavy kettle or Dutch oven. Add water, broth granules, *1 teaspoon* (5 ml) salt, fines herbes and pepper. Bring to a boil. Cover; simmer 1 to 1½ hours until meat is very tender. Skim excess fat. Add Hunt's Sauce, vegetables and *remaining* salt. Simmer, covered, about 30 minutes until carrots are tender. Makes 6 servings,

Or use 3 lbs. (1400 g) beef neck bones or 2 lbs. (900 g) beef shank slices.

Delicious Low-cost Dishes FRANK 'N MAC CASSEROLE

Non-fat dry milk makes it extra nutritious

225 g	½ lb. frankfurters, sliced in 1-inch (3 cm) pieces
125 ml	½ cup minced onion
125 ml	½ cup minced green pepper
15 ml	1 Tablesp. margarine
225 g	½ lb. shell macaroni
180 ml	¾ cup instant non-fat dry milk
375 ml	1½ cups water
3 ml	½ teasp. salt
1 ml	¼ teasp. thyme
	1 (8-oz./226 g) can Hunt's Tomato Sauce
375 ml	1½ cups diced process American cheese

Sauté frankfurters, onion and green pepper in margarine in large skillet until onion is soft. Cook macaroni in boiling salted water according to package directions; drain well. Add to skillet mixture. Stir in non-fat dry milk, water, salt and thyme; continue stirring gently over low heat to blend thoroughly. Stir in Hunt's Sauce and *1 cup* (250 ml) cheese. Pour into 2-quart (2 liter) casserole or baking dish. Bake at 350° (175°C) 20 minutes. Top with *remaining* cheese; bake 10 minutes longer. Makes 6 to 8 servings.

Opposite: Frank 'n Mac Casserole

Delicious Low-cost Dishes HAM-IT-UP SOUP[C]

Full-flavored and hearty as an entrée soup

450 g	1	lb. lentils
2.5 l	2½	qts. water
	2	ham hocks or 1 meaty ham bone
250 ml	1	cup chopped celery
	1	carrot, chopped
	1	(15-oz./425 g) can Hunt's Tomato Sauce with Tomato Bits
5 ml	1	teasp. Worcestershire
3 ml	½	teasp. *each:* salt and seasoned salt
1 ml	¼	teasp. pepper

In Dutch oven or kettle, combine all ingredients; bring to a
boil. Simmer, covered, for 2 hours, stirring occasionally.
Remove skin and bone from ham; skim off fat from broth.
Return meat to soup. Makes 6 to 8 servings.

[C]*Slow Cooker*

Delicious Low-cost Dishes PANHANDLER'S CHILI BEEF[C]

A long-overlooked meat-cut bargain

1400 g	3	lbs. meaty beef neck bones
		Salt and pepper
		Water
	2	(8-oz./226 g) cans Hunt's Tomato Sauce
	1	clove garlic, minced
15 ml	1	Tablesp. chili powder
1 ml	¼	teasp. oregano
	1	(1-lb. 14-oz./850 g) can small red beans, undrained

Sprinkle beef neck bones with salt
and pepper; place in large casserole
or baking dish with *1 cup (250
ml)* water. Cover and bake 1½
to 2 hours at 325° (165°C)
until meat falls away from
bones. Remove bones;
strain broth, adding *enough
water,* if necessary, *to make
1 cup (250 ml)* broth. Combine
with meat, Hunt's Sauce and
remaining ingredients in large
kettle. Simmer 20 to 30
minutes until desired consistency;
stir occasionally. Makes 6 servings.

*The succulent pieces
of meat from either
beef or pork neck
bones are marvelous
in all manners of
casseroles, sandwich
fillings and soups.*

[C]*Slow Cooker*

Delicious Low-cost Dishes

DEVILED EGGS EN CASSEROLE
Extra-pretty in individual baking dishes

	2 (8-oz./226 g) cans Hunt's Tomato Sauce
430 ml	1¾ cups water
30 ml	2 Tablesp. butter or margarine
	1 (6-oz./170 g) pkg. quick-cooking Spanish rice
	6 hard-cooked eggs
45 ml	3 Tablesp. mayonnaise
15 ml	1 Tablesp. minced green onion
5 ml	1 teasp. prepared mustard
3 ml	½ teasp. seasoned salt
.5 ml	⅛ teasp. pepper
375 ml	1½ cups shredded Cheddar cheese

Combine *1 can* Hunt's Sauce, water, butter and seasoning packet from Spanish rice mix in saucepan; bring to a boil. Stir in rice; cover, let stand 10 minutes. Meanwhile, cut eggs in half lengthwise. Remove yolks and mash in small bowl with mayonnaise, onion, mustard, salt and pepper. Use to fill egg white halves; set aside. Stir *1 cup* (250 ml) cheese and *remaining can* Hunt's Sauce into prepared Spanish rice; place in bottom of buttered 7½- x 12- x 1½-inch (18 x 30 x 4 cm) baking dish. Arrange stuffed egg halves over top, sprinkle with *remaining* cheese. Bake at 375° (190°C) 20 minutes. Makes 4 to 6 servings. (See photo page 125)

Delicious Low-cost Dishes

SPOONBREAD OLE
A southern favorite

125 ml	½ cup chopped onion
30 ml	2 Tablesp. butter
	1 (8-oz./226 g) can Hunt's Tomato Sauce
125 ml	½ cup yellow cornmeal
250 ml	1 cup water
125 ml	½ cup shredded sharp Cheddar cheese
5 ml	1 teasp. salt
	2 eggs, well beaten
30 ml	2 Tablesp. diced canned green chilies

In 1-quart (1 liter) saucepan, sauté onion in butter until onion is soft. Add Hunt's Sauce; bring to a simmer. Stir cornmeal into water; pour into simmering sauce mixture, stirring constantly. Continue cooking, stirring, until mixture is consistency of thick mush. Remove from heat. Add cheese and salt; mix thoroughly. Stir in beaten eggs and green chilies. Pour into 1-quart (1 liter) buttered casserole. Bake at 425° (220°C) 45 minutes. Serve at once. Makes 4 to 5 servings.

Delicious Low-cost Dishes **BAKED TUNA SALAD SOUFFLE**

Perfect for a party lunch or family supper

	1 (7-oz./198 g) can solid white tuna
125 ml	½ cup minced onion
125 ml	½ cup minced celery
60 ml	¼ cup minced green pepper
	6 slices French bread, ½ inch (1 cm) thick
60 ml	¼ cup mayonnaise
115 g	¼ lb. Cheddar cheese, diced
	4 eggs, slightly beaten
250 ml	1 cup milk
	1 (8-oz./226 g) can Hunt's Tomato Sauce with Cheese
3 ml	½ teasp. seasoned salt

Drain oil from tuna into small skillet. Add onion, celery and green pepper and sauté until onion is soft. Add tuna and toss to mix; set aside. Spread bread slices with mayonnaise; cut into small cubes. In a buttered 1½ quart (1.5 liter) casserole, arrange layers of *half* the bread cubes, *half* the tuna mixture and *half* the cheese. Repeat layers, using *remaining* bread cubes, tuna mixture and cheese. Combine eggs in a bowl with milk; stir in Hunt's Sauce gradually and add seasoned salt; mix well. Pour slowly over casserole, pressing gently to immerse all ingredients; let stand 10 minutes. Bake at 350° (175°C) 1 hour until golden brown and puffed on top. Makes 6 servings.

Delicious Low-cost Dishes **JIFFY FRANK-A-RONI**

Package dinner quickie to the rescue

	1 (7¼-oz./205 g) pkg. macaroni and cheese dinner
60 ml	¼ cup chopped onion
	1 (8-oz./226 g) can Hunt's Tomato Sauce
	1 (10-oz./283 g) pkg. frozen mixed vegetables, thawed
3 ml	½ teasp. salt
225 g	½ lb. frankfurters
125 ml	½ cup shredded cheese

In large saucepan, prepare macaroni and cheese dinner according to package directions. Stir in onion, Hunt's Sauce, mixed vegetables and salt. Bring to a boil; stir. Pour into greased 6- x 10- x 1½-inch (15 x 25 x 4 cm) baking dish. Arrange frankfurters over top. Sprinkle with cheese. Bake at 325° (165°C) 25 to 30 minutes. Makes 4 servings.

BRAISED LAMB SHANKS CONTINENTAL

Delicious and handsome entrée

	4 lamb shanks
	1 clove garlic, slivered
60 ml	¼ cup pure vegetable oil
	Salt and pepper
	1 (8-oz./226 g) can Hunt's Tomato Sauce with Onions
125 ml	½ cup dry white wine
60 ml	¼ cup water
15 ml	1 Tablesp. Worcestershire
15 ml	1 Tablesp. brown sugar, packed
3 ml	½ teasp. basil
	Chopped parsley

With a sharp knife, cut several deep slits into meaty part of each lamb shank; insert slivers of garlic. Brown shanks lightly on all sides in oil in large skillet; drain excess fat. Sprinkle shanks on all sides with salt and pepper. Combine remaining ingredients, *except* parsley; pour over browned shanks. Cover; simmer gently about 1½ hours until fork-tender. Turn once or twice during cooking. Skim excess fat, if necessary. Sprinkle with parsley just before serving. Makes 4 servings.

DUTCH-OVEN PINTOS

A flavorful change from familiar navy beans

500 ml	2 cups dry pinto or pink beans
1250 ml	5 cups water
	Salt
	2 (about 1 lb./450 g) fresh pork hocks
	1 onion, chopped
	1 (8-oz./226 g) can Hunt's Tomato Sauce
60 ml	¼ cup brown sugar, packed
3 ml	½ teasp. dry mustard
.5 ml	⅛ teasp. marjoram (optional)

Wash beans; place in Dutch oven or large kettle. Add water, bring to a boil for 2 minutes; cover and let stand 2 hours. Drain; rinse beans; add fresh water to cover, *1 teaspoon* (5 ml) salt and pork hocks, washed but unskinned. Bring to a boil; simmer, covered, 1 hour. Remove skin and bones from hocks, return meat to beans; stir in *½ teaspoon* (3 ml) salt and remaining ingredients. Cover, simmer about 1½ hours until meat and beans are tender. Stir occasionally. Makes 6 to 8 servings.

POLYNESIAN STEAK TWIST-UPS
Feature at a dinner party, expect compliments

	1 flank steak (about 1½ lbs./675 g)
	1 (8-oz./226 g) can Hunt's Tomato Sauce with Onions
60 ml	¼ cup brown sugar
60 ml	¼ cup soy sauce
3 ml	½ teasp. ground ginger
	1 (13½-oz./375 g) can pineapple chunks, undrained
	Bamboo skewers
	1 green pepper, cut into 1-inch (3 cm) pieces
	1 (6-oz./170 g) can water chestnuts, halved
750 ml	3 cups hot cooked rice

Cut steak crosswise into thin 1-inch-wide (3 cm) strips, set aside. Combine Hunt's Sauce, sugar, soy sauce, ginger and ¼ cup (60 ml) pineapple juice in 9- x 13- 1½-inch (23 x 33 x 4 cm) baking dish. Lace steak strips on skewers with 3 to 4 pieces each of pineapple, green pepper and water chestnuts. Arrange in baking dish with marinade, turning to coat all sides. Let stand at least 1 hour, turning skewers occasionally. Place skewer-twist-ups on grill 2 inches (5 ml) above very hot coals. Cook 10 to 12 minutes, turning every 2 to 3 minutes; baste often with remaining marinade. Add any remaining pieces of water chestnuts to hot cooked rice. Arrange twist-ups on rice. Makes 6 servings.

Because it's solid meat with no fat or bone, flank steak is a great serving stretcher.

POTLUCK BEAN BAKE
Right off the shelf for an emergency casserole

	1 (1-lb./450 g) can pork and beans, undrained
	1 (15-oz./425 g) can pinto beans, drained
	1 (15-oz./425 g) can chili beans, drained
225 g	½ lb. frankfurters, diagonally sliced
	1 8-oz./226 g) can Hunt's Tomato Sauce with Onions
30 ml	2 Tablesp. brown sugar, packed
15 ml	1 Tablesp. Worcestershire
5 ml	1 teasp. prepared mustard

Combine all ingredients in a 7½- x 12- x 1½-inch (18 x 30 x 4 cm) baking dish. Mix thoroughly. Bake, uncovered, at 375° (190°C) 30 to 35 minutes. Makes 6 to 8 servings.

STUFFED SHOULDER OF LAMB
Just as beautiful as a higher-priced cut

1500 g	3- to 4-lb lamb shoulder roast with pocket*
5 ml	1 teasp. salt
.5 ml	⅛ teasp. pepper
85 ml	⅓ cup *each:* diced celery and onion
45 ml	3 Tablesp. margarine or butter
125 ml	½ cup soft bread crumbs
60 ml	¼ cup raisins
5 ml	1 teasp. oregano
	1 clove garlic, crushed
	1 (8-oz./226 g) can Hunt's Tomato Sauce

Sprinkle roast with salt and pepper. Cook celery and onion in margarine in small skillet until transparent. Add bread crumbs and raisins; toss lightly. Stir oregano and garlic into Hunt's Sauce; add ⅓ *cup* (85 ml) to stuffing mixture. Use to fill pocket in roast; seal open edges with skewers or tie with twine. Roast on rack in shallow pan at 325° (165°C) 2 hours. Drain excess fat. Pour remaining Hunt's Sauce mixture over roast. Roast 30 to 40 minutes longer; baste often. Makes 6 to 8 servings.

*For easier carving, have your butcher remove the blade bone.

MACARONI AND CHEESE LOAF
An old favorite with a whole new look

375 ml	1½ cups elbow macaroni
125 ml	½ cup milk
375 ml	1½ cups shredded Cheddar cheese
60 ml	¼ cup *each:* minced onion and green pepper
30 ml	2 Tablesp. pure vegetable oil
125 ml	½ cup soft bread crumbs
	1 (15-oz./425 g) can Hunt's Tomato Sauce with Tomato Bits
	3 eggs, well beaten
3 ml	½ teasp. salt

Cook macaroni in boiling salted water according to package directions; drain. Add milk and cheese, stir until well blended. Meanwhile, cook onion and green pepper in oil in small skillet until soft; add bread crumbs, stir to coat. Add to macaroni mixture; stir in Hunt's Sauce, beaten eggs and salt; mix thoroughly. Spoon into well-greased 9- x 5- x 3-inch (23 x 13 x 8 cm) loaf pan. Bake at 350° (175°C) 50 to 55 minutes until set. Let stand 10 minutes; turn out on serving platter. Serve slices with ketchup, if desired. Makes 6 to 8 servings.

Delicious Low-cost Dishes CHICKEN LIVERS, CREOLE STYLE
Wonderfully nutritious and fantastically delicious

625 ml	2½	cups water
	3	chicken bouillon cubes
250 ml	1	cup uncooked rice
60 ml	¼	cup chopped green onion tops
	2	slices bacon, diced
450 g	1	lb. chicken livers
30 ml	2	Tablesp. flour
3 ml	½	teasp. seasoned salt
.5 ml	⅛	teasp. pepper
	1	(15-oz./425 g) can Hunt's Tomato Sauce Special
30 ml	2	Tablesp. chopped parsley

Bring water and bouillon cubes to a boil in 1-quart (1 liter) saucepan. Stir in rice; cover, simmer 20 minutes. Remove from heat; stir in green onions. Cover; let stand 5 minutes. Meanwhile, fry bacon until crisp in 10-inch (25 cm) skillet; remove and reserve. Dust chicken livers with flour; sauté in bacon drippings in skillet 3 to 5 minutes, turning livers until golden on all sides. Sprinkle with salt and pepper. Add Hunt's Sauce and reserved bacon; simmer, uncovered, about 5 minutes. Serve over hot cooked rice; sprinkle with parsley. Makes 4 to 6 servings.

Delicious Low-cost Dishes SAUCY LITTLE LOAVES
Individual portions beautifully glazed

675 g	1½	lbs. lean ground beef
	1	egg
125 ml	½	cup quick-cooking oats
60 ml	¼	cup minced onion
8 ml	1½	teasp. salt
1 ml	¼	teasp. pepper
	2	(8-oz./226 g) cans Hunt's Tomato Sauce with Mushrooms
60 ml	¼	cup orange marmalade
5 ml	1	teasp. Worcestershire

In bowl, combine ground beef with *next 5* ingredients and *½ cup* (125 ml) Hunt's Sauce. Shape into 6 oval loaves in shallow baking dish. Bake at 450° (230°C) 20 minutes. Combine *remaining* Hunt's Sauce, marmalade and Worcestershire in small bowl. At end of baking time, remove excess fat from pan and pour sauce mixture over loaves. Bake 10 minutes longer. Makes 6 servings.

Delicious Low-cost Dishes CHILI DOGS

Popular with any age group indoors or out

225 g	½ lb. ground beef
250 ml	1 cup chopped onion
10 ml	2 teasp. chili powder
3 ml	½ teasp. salt
	1 (8-oz./226 g) can Hunt's Tomato Sauce
	8 hot dogs
	8 hot dog buns, split
180 ml	¾ cup shredded Cheddar cheese

Cook ground beef and *½ cup* (125 ml) onion in small skillet until beef loses redness and onion is transparent; drain fat. Add chili powder, salt and Hunt's Sauce; mix well. Simmer 5 minutes. Meanwhile, heat or grill hot dogs and buns. Place hot dogs in buns. Spoon chili down center of each; top each with *remaining* onion and shredded cheese. Makes 8 chili dogs.

Delicious Low-cost Dishes SPLIT PEAS, PLANTATION STYLE[C]

Serve with homemade bread for a special budget treat

250 ml	1 cup dry split peas
	Water
5 ml	1 teasp. salt
115 g	¼ lb. diced salt pork, bacon or ham scraps
	1 onion, coarsely chopped
125 ml	½ cup diced carrots
	1 (15-oz./425 g) can Hunt's Tomato Sauce Special
1 ml	¼ teasp. ginger

In kettle, cover peas with *2 cups* (500 ml) water; bring to boil for 2 minutes. Add salt; cover, set aside for ½ hour. Meanwhile, in small skillet cook salt pork and onion until onion is transparent. Add to peas along with remaining ingredients and *3 more cups* (750 ml) water. Bring to a boil; boil gently 1 hour. Serve in soup plates. Makes 4 servings.

Split peas, lentils, dry navy and lima beans are all economical foods especially high in protein.

[C]*Slow Cooker*

A Potpourri of Tomato Sauce Treats

Tomato sauce is one of the most versatile foods in the world. And if you don't believe it now, you will after you try the marvelous recipes in this chapter.

It's got everything from sandwiches and salads to soups, appetizers, a quick bread and more. A veritable potpourri of tasty, tantalizing tomato sauce treats.

MEATBALL SUBMARINES
For early or late suppers, a super sandwich

900 g	2	lbs. ground beef and pork for meat loaf
	2	eggs
125 ml	½	cup Italian-flavored bread crumbs
		Grated Romano or Parmesan cheese
30 ml	2	Tablesp. parsley flakes
		Oregano
3 ml	½	teasp. salt
30 ml	2	Tablesp. pure vegetable oil
	2	(15-oz./425 g) cans Hunt's Tomato Herb Sauce
	8	large French rolls
		Butter

In large mixing bowl, thoroughly combine ground meats, eggs, bread crumbs, ½ cup (125 ml) grated Romano or Parmesan cheese, parsley flakes, ¼ teaspoon (1 ml) oregano and salt. Shape into 40 (1½ inch/4 cm) meatballs. Brown in oil in a 12-inch (30 cm) skillet over medium heat, turning meatballs to brown on all sides; drain fat. Add ½ teaspoon (3 ml) oregano to Hunt's Sauce; pour over meatballs. Cover and simmer 15 minutes. Meanwhile, split and butter rolls; wrap in foil and heat at 350° (175°C) 15 minutes. To serve, place 5 meatballs and a spoonful of sauce on each roll. Sprinkle with additional grated cheese. Makes 8 sandwiches.

MACARONI SUPPER SALAD
Hearty enough for the main dish, pretty enough for a patio party

	1	(8-oz./225 g) pkg. small shell macaroni
500 ml	2	cups diced cooked ham or luncheon meat
125 ml	½	cup coarsely grated raw carrot
60 ml	¼	cup chopped onion
60 ml	¼	cup chopped green pepper
5 ml	1	teasp. salt
250 ml	1	cup mayonnaise or salad dressing
	1	(8-oz./226 g) can Hunt's Tomato Sauce

Cook, drain and rinse macaroni according to package directions. Mix with ham, carrot, onion, green pepper and salt in large bowl. Blend mayonnaise and Hunt's Sauce in small bowl. Pour over salad ingredients; toss lightly to mix. Chill thoroughly. Serve on crisp salad greens. Makes 6 servings.

A Potpourri of Tomato Sauce Treats

SPICY SHRIMP LUNCHEON MOLD
A sparkling salad with a refreshing flavor

	2 (15-oz./425 g) cans Hunt's Tomato Sauce with Tomato Bits
	1 (6-oz./170 g) pkg. raspberry-flavored gelatin
5 ml	1 teasp. instant minced onion
5 ml	1 teasp. celery seed
5 ml	1 teasp. salt
4 ml	¾ teasp. prepared horseradish
.5 ml	⅛ teasp. cayenne
	3 drops Tabasco
375 ml	1½ cups shredded cabbage
125 ml	½ cup sweet pickle relish
450 g	1 lb. small cooked shrimp or 2 (4.5-oz./128 g) cans shrimp, drained

In a medium saucepan, bring Hunt's Sauce to a boil. Add raspberry-flavored gelatin and stir until dissolved. Add onion, celery seed, salt, horseradish, cayenne and Tabasco. Cool. Add cabbage, relish and shrimp. Pour into a 7-cup (1750 ml) mold. Chill until firm. Unmold on bed of greens. Serve with sour cream. Makes 6 to 8 servings.

A Potpourri of Tomato Sauce Treats

QUICK-BREAD CHEESE LOAF
For an extra treat, try it toasted

1000 ml	4 cups all-purpose baking mix
250 ml	1 cup shredded Cheddar cheese
30 ml	2 Tablesp. dill seed
	1 (8-oz./226 g) can Hunt's Tomato Sauce with Onions
125 ml	½ cup milk
60 ml	¼ cup mayonnaise

Combine all ingredients in mixing bowl; stir until just blended. Turn into greased 9- x 5- x 3-inch (23 x 13 x 8 cm) loaf pan or 6- x 10- x 1½-inch (15 x 25 x 4 cm) baking dish. Bake at 350° (175°C) 45 to 55 minutes, until a toothpick inserted in center comes out clean. Makes 1 loaf.

Opposite: Spicy Shrimp Luncheon Mold

CHILLED CREAM OF TOMATO SOUP
A sensational first course soup

A Potpourri of Tomato Sauce Treats

	1 (½-oz./14 g) env. bacon and onion or green onion dip mix
125 ml	½ cup imitation sour cream
	1 (15-oz./425 g) can Hunt's Tomato Sauce with Tomato Bits
	4 slices bacon, fried, drained well and crumbled
3 ml	½ teasp. sweet basil leaves, crushed
60 ml	¼ cup dry white wine
	3 (10½-oz./298 g) cans chicken broth
	3 drops Tabasco
	12 crescent slices of avocado

In large bowl, blend together dip mix, sour cream, Hunt's Sauce, bacon and basil; mix well. Slowly stir in wine, chicken broth and Tabasco; chill thoroughly. Serve in individual icers; garnish each with avocado crescent. Makes 6 luncheon or 12 small first-course servings.

SAVORY MARINADE
Use this all-purpose sauce for steak, hamburgers, chicken, pork and ribs

A Potpourri of Tomato Sauce Treats

125 ml	½ cup chopped green onions
	3 cloves garlic, minced
15 ml	1 Tablesp. pure vegetable oil
	2 (8-oz./226 g) or 1 (15-oz./425 g) can Hunt's Tomato Sauce
125 ml	½ cup wine vinegar
60 ml	¼ cup molasses
5 ml	1 teasp. *each:* celery salt, chili powder, dry mustard and bouquet garni
1500 g	3 to 4 lbs. sirloin tip steak, ¾ inch (2 cm) thick

Sauté onions and garlic in vegetable oil in 10-inch (25 cm) skillet until golden. Add remaining ingredients, *except* steak; mix thoroughly. Place steak in shallow baking dish(es); pour above mixture over steak and marinate at least 3 hours, turning once. Remove steak from marinade. Broil 3 to 4 inches (8 to 10 cm) from heat source 6 minutes per side for rare; baste occasionally. Makes about 2½ cups (625 ml) marinade.

Opposite: Savory Marinade

TOMATO FRENCH DRESSING

Keep this on hand for savory mixed green or seafood salads

	1 (8-oz./226 g) can Hunt's Tomato Sauce
125 ml	½ cup pure vegetable oil
60 ml	¼ cup vinegar
15 ml	1 Tablesp. sugar
3 ml	½ teasp. salt
1 ml	¼ teasp. dry mustard
.5 ml	⅛ teasp. garlic salt

Combine all ingredients in a cruet or jar. Shake well and refrigerate. Makes about 2 cups (500 ml) dressing.

Allow refrigerated salad dressings to stand at room temperature half an hour before serving for perfect blending and full flavor.

HUNT'S HAWAIIAN SAUCE

A popular sauce with a very special flavor

60 ml	¼ cup brown sugar, packed
10 ml	2 teasp. cornstarch
	1 (8-oz./226 g) can Hunt's Tomato Sauce
	1 (8½-oz./240 g) can crushed pineapple, undrained
30 ml	1 Tablesp. lemon juice
30 ml	1 Tablesp. minced crystallized ginger
1 ml	¼ teasp. onion salt
1 ml	¼ teasp. garlic salt
.5 ml	⅛ teasp. pepper

Blend brown sugar and cornstarch in 1-quart (1 liter) saucepan. Add remaining ingredients; blend thoroughly. Bring to a boil, stirring. Lower heat; cover, simmer gently 15 to 20 minutes. Stir occasionally. Use as basting or serving sauce for chicken, ribs, meatballs. Makes 2 cups (500 ml) sauce.

HOMEMADE SLOPPY JOES
Great-for a crowd or a family make-ahead

1400 g	3	lbs. ground beef
8 ml	1½	teasp. salt
3 ml	½	teasp. pepper
375 ml	1½	cups chopped onion
125 ml	½	cup chopped green pepper
125 ml	½	cup chopped celery
	2	(15-oz./425 g) or 1 (29-oz./822 g) can Hunt's Tomato Sauce
250 ml	1	cup water
125 ml	½	cup ketchup
30 ml	2	Tablesp. Worcestershire
15 ml	1	Tablesp. prepared mustard
15 ml	1	to 2 Tablesp. brown sugar, packed
	20	hamburger buns

Cook beef in large kettle or Dutch oven until it loses redness. Drain excess fat. Add salt, pepper, onion, green pepper and celery; cook, stirring occasionally, about 5 minutes to soften vegetables. Stir in remaining ingredients, *except* buns; simmer 10 to 15 minutes, stirring occasionally, until desired consistency. Serve between buns. Makes about 20 Sloppy Joes, *or:* freeze in family-size portions.

OUT-OF-SIGHT BEAN DIP
Heats in the oven while you're the carefree hostess

	1	(1-lb. 4-oz./567 g) can refried beans
	1	(8-oz./226 g) can Hunt's Tomato Sauce
225 g	½	lb. jack cheese, diced
125 ml	½	cup finely minced onion
30 ml	2	to 3 Tablesp. diced canned green chilies
15 ml	1	Tablesp. chili powder
	1	(10-oz./283 g) pkg. tortilla chips
		Pitted whole ripe olives (optional)

Combine refried beans, Hunt's Sauce, diced cheese, onion, chilies and chili powder with ⅓ cup *crushed* (85 ml) tortilla chips in 1½ quart (1.5 liter) casserole; mix well. Bake, uncovered, at 375° (190°C) 35 to 40 minutes until hot and bubbly. Stir with spoon to swirl cheese through mixture. Press some tortilla chips in two rows around outer edge of casserole; garnish with ripe olives, if desired. Serve with bowl of remaining chips. Makes about 1 quart (1 liter) of dip.

144

GAZPACHO

As tasty as the popular Mexican restaurant specialty

	1 (15-oz./425 g) can Hunt's Tomato Sauce with Tomato Bits
	1 (2-oz./56 g) can pimientos, drained and chopped
	1 medium green pepper, chopped
	½ cucumber, diced
	1 clove garlic, minced
30 ml	2 Tablesp. pure vegetable oil
30 ml	2 Tablesp. wine vinegar
5 ml	1 teasp. salt
5 ml	1 teasp. sugar
.5 ml	⅛ to ¼ teasp. Tabasco
125 ml	½ cup croutons

Combine all ingredients, *except* croutons; chill thoroughly. Serve in chilled small soup bowls or glasses; garnish with croutons. Make 6 (½-cup/125 ml) servings.

Like garlic, but not that much? Spear a whole peeled clove on a toothpick and add to recipe until you have the flavor you want, then remove.

HUNT'S BLOODY MARY

The great morning eye-opener

	2 (8-oz./226 g) cans Hunt's Tomato Sauce
250 ml	1 cup water
180 ml	¾ cup vodka
23 ml	1½ Tablesp. lemon juice
5 ml	1 teasp. Worcestershire
	4 drops Tabasco
5 ml	1 teasp. celery salt
3 ml	½ teasp. salt
	6 small leafy ribs of celery

In large pitcher, blend all ingredients together, *except* celery. Serve over crushed ice in glasses. Garnish with celery. Makes (3½ cups/875 ml) 4 to 6 servings.

A Potpourri of Tomato Sauce Treats
TOMATO MUSHROOM SOUP
A cupboard shelf standby

	2 (8-oz./226 g) cans Hunt's Tomato Sauce with Mushrooms
3 ml	½ teasp. baking soda
3 ml	½ teasp. seasoned salt
	1 (2½-oz./64 g) can broiled-in-butter mushrooms, undrained
500 ml	2 cups milk

In medium saucepan, combine Hunt's Sauce, soda, seasoned salt and mushrooms. (Mixture will be foamy.) Gradually stir in milk. Cook over low heat, stirring frequently, until heated through. Makes 4 servings.

A Potpourri of Tomato Sauce Treats
APPLE-TOMATO CHUTNEY
A gourmet touch for meats

500 ml	2 cups chopped pared tart apples
125 ml	½ cup chopped onion
250 ml	1 cup seedless raisins
	1 (8-oz./226 g) can Hunt's Tomato Sauce
250 ml	1 cup brown sugar, packed
125 ml	½ cup vinegar
10 ml	2 teasp. salt
15 ml	1 Tablesp. chopped candied ginger

Combine all ingredients in heavy saucepan. Cook slowly, uncovered, *1 hour;* stir occasionally. Chill. Serve as condiment with poultry, beef or game. Makes 2 cups (500 ml).

A Potpourri of Tomato Sauce Treats
SAUCED-UP SMOKIES
These will keep the appetizer crowd happy.

	1 (8-oz./226 g) can Hunt's Tomato Sauce
	1 (1¼-oz./35 g) pkg. dry onion soup mix
	2 (12-oz./340 g) pkgs. smoky link sausages, cut into bite-size pieces
250 ml	1 cup sour cream

In medium saucepan, combine Hunt's Sauce and onion soup mix. Add smoky link pieces and heat through. Stir in sour cream. Keep warm for serving but do not boil. For easy eating, place a toothpick in each piece of sausage. Makes about 16 appetizer servings.

New Ways To Serve Ground Beef

For reasons
of economy, ease and most
of all taste, hamburger and
Hunt's Tomato Sauce have always
been a terrific combination. The flavor
of one brings out and enhances the
flavor of the other.

So in this chapter, we've included some
very new ways to combine these two old
favorites. There are sixteen ingenious
recipe ideas that both your family
and friends will adore.

MACARONI AND CHEESE PIZZA
A uniquely different pizza taste

	1	(8-oz./225 g) pkg. elbow macaroni
	1	(10-oz./305 g) can condensed Cheddar cheese soup
60 ml	¼	cup *each:* minced onion and green pepper
	3	eggs, well beaten
5 ml	1	teasp. oregano
5 ml	1	teasp. sweet basil
3 ml	½	teasp. salt
3 ml	½	teasp. garlic powder
	1	(15-oz./425 g) can Hunt's Tomato Sauce
125 ml	½	cup shredded Cheddar cheese
225 g	½	lb. ground beef, cooked and crumbled

Cook macaroni according to package directions; drain thoroughly. Add soup, onion, green pepper and eggs; mix well. Spread in greased 14-inch (36 cm) pizza pan or two 9-inch (23 cm) pie plates. Bake at 350° (175°C) 25 minutes. Add seasonings to Hunt's Sauce; pour over macaroni and spread evenly. Sprinkle on cheese and crumbled beef. Bake 10 minutes longer. Makes 6 to 8 servings.

STUFFED ACORN SQUASH^M
Savory meat filling and tender, golden squash

	3	small acorn squash, halved and seeded
		Salt and pepper
450 g	1	lb. ground beef
	1	(8-oz./226 g) can Hunt's Tomato Sauce
125 ml	½	cup soft bread crumbs
125 ml	½	cup chopped green pepper
15 ml	1	Tablesp. minced parsley
15 ml	1	Tablesp. instant minced onion

Sprinkle squash with salt and pepper. Turn cut side down on lightly greased jelly roll pan or large glass baking dish. Bake squash at 350° (175°C) 30 minutes. In a bowl, combine ground beef with remaining ingredients; mix thoroughly. Turn partially cooked squash cut side up. Fill centers with meat mixture. Bake 30 minutes longer or until squash is tender. Makes 6 servings.

ᴹ*Microwave*

New Ways To Serve Ground Beef

CHECKERBOARD BEEF BITES
An easy oven-do party appetizer

900 g	2 lbs. lean ground beef
500 ml	2 cups soft bread crumbs
125 ml	½ cup finely minced onion
30 ml	2 Tablesp. Worcestershire
5 ml	1 teasp. salt
1 ml	¼ teasp. pepper
	2 cloves garlic, crushed
	1 (8-oz./226 g) can Hunt's Tomato Sauce
15 ml	1 Tablesp. brown sugar
10 ml	2 teasp. prepared horseradish

Toppings
Sliced pimiento-stuffed or pitted ripe olives
Sliced sweet gherkins or cocktail onions
Diced Cheddar cheese

In a bowl, combine ground beef with next 6 ingredients and ½ cup (125 ml) Hunt's Sauce; mix thoroughly. Form into two rectangles about 5- x 10-inches (13 x 25 cm) each on shallow baking or jelly roll pan. Mark each into 30 squares by pressing a kitchen knife through meat almost to bottom of pan. Bake at 425° (220°C) 10 minutes; drain fat. Add brown sugar and horseradish to *remainder* of Hunt's Sauce. Use to brush on partially baked beef squares. Arrange suggested toppings in center of squares, checkerboard fashion; bake 5 minutes longer. Cut apart to serve. Makes 60 bite-size appetizers.

New Ways To Serve Ground Beef

MEXICANA CASSEROLE
Taco seasoning mix adds the delicious flavor

675 g	1½ lbs. ground beef
	1 onion, chopped
	1 large clove garlic, minced
	1 pkg. (about 2 oz./56 g) taco seasoning mix
	1 (15-oz./425 g) can Hunt's Tomato Sauce
250 ml	1 cup water
	1 pkg. (about 20 oz./610 g) corn tortillas
625 ml	2½ cups shredded Cheddar cheese

Sauté ground beef, onions and garlic in 10-inch (25 cm) skillet until beef loses redness; drain fat. Add taco seasoning, Hunt's Sauce and water; simmer 3 to 5 minutes. In a 2-quart (2 liter) casserole, arrange alternate layers of tortillas, meat sauce and cheese until all used up. Bake at 350° (175°C) 30 to 40 minutes. Makes 6 to 8 servings.

MEATBALL FONDUE
Meatballs dressed up for a party

450 g	1	lb. ground beef
250 ml	1	cup soft bread crumbs
	1	egg, beaten
5 ml	1	teasp. instant minced onion
4 ml	¾	teasp. seasoned salt
1 ml	¼	teasp. garlic powder
	1	(8-oz./226 g) can Hunt's Tomato Sauce
30 ml	2	Tablesp. red wine
	1	(2-oz./56 g) can mushrooms, drained and chopped
5 ml	1	teasp. minced parsley
5 ml	1	teasp. sugar
		Pure vegetable oil

In medium bowl, thoroughly combine first 6 ingredients and *2 tablespoons* Hunt's Sauce. Form mixture into 36 (1-inch/3 cm) meatballs. Combine *remaining* Hunt's Sauce and *remaining* ingredients *except* oil in a saucepan. Bring to a boil. Keep warm. Heat *2 to 3 cups* (500 to 750 ml) oil to 375° (190°C)* in 1½ quart (1.5 liter) heavy saucepan or electric fondue pot. Spear meatballs on skewers or fondue forks; immerse in hot oil about 1½ minutes. Dip in sauce to serve. Makes 4 servings.

Always use a frying thermometer for accurate temperature control and safety.

BEEF-POTATO BOATS ^M
Popular new way to serve meat and potatoes

450 g	1	lb. ground beef
125 ml	½	cup chopped celery
30 ml	2	Tablesp. diced canned green chilies
5 ml	1	teasp. salt
1 ml	¼	teasp. nutmeg
	1	(8-oz./226 g) can Hunt's Tomato Sauce with Onions
375 ml	1½	cups shredded Cheddar cheese
	4	medium-sized potatoes, baked

Brown ground beef and celery in skillet. Drain fat. Add chilies, salt, nutmeg, Hunt's Sauce and *1 cup* (250 ml) cheese. Cut potatoes in half lengthwise. Scoop out and reserve shells. Mash potatoes. Combine with meat mixture. Use to fill shells. Place in baking pan. Sprinkle with *remaining* cheese. Bake at 400° (205°C) 15 minutes. Makes 4 servings.

M*Microwave*

New Ways To Serve Ground Beef

30-MINUTE HAMBURGER SOUP^M

A main dish soup that tastes like it cooked hours.

450 g	1 lb. ground beef
	1 medium onion, chopped
250 ml	1 cup chopped celery (with tops)
125 ml	½ cup chopped parsley
10 ml	2 teasp. salt
5 ml	1 teasp. Worcestershire
5 ml	1 teasp. seasoned salt
1 ml	¼ teasp. pepper
	2 (8-oz./226 g) cans Hunt's Tomato Sauce with Mushrooms
750 ml	3 cups water
	1 (10-oz./285 g) pkg. frozen mixed vegetables

In Dutch oven or kettle, cook beef, onion and celery until beef is browned and onion is tender. Drain fat. Add remaining ingredients; simmer, covered, 20 to 25 minutes or until vegetables are tender. Makes 6 (about 1½ -cup/375 ml) servings.

^M*Microwave*

New Ways To Serve Ground Beef

CALIFORNIA CONEYS^M

The best of East and West combine to make this tasty treat.

	1 medium onion, chopped
60 ml	¼ cup chopped green pepper
225 g	½ lb. ground beef
	1 (8-oz./226 g) can Hunt's Tomato Sauce
85 ml	⅓ cup sweet pickle relish
5 ml	1 teasp. prepared mustard
5 ml	1 teasp. Worcestershire
5 ml	1 teasp. salt
	8 hot dogs
	8 hot dog buns, split, toasted and buttered
250 ml	1 cup shredded sharp Cheddar cheese

Cook onion and green pepper with ground beef in small skillet until beef loses redness and onion softens slightly. Drain fat. Stir in Hunt's Sauce, pickle relish, mustard, Worcestershire and salt. Arrange hot dogs in meat sauce; simmer about 10 minutes, turning hot dogs once or twice. Place hot dogs down center of toasted buns. Spoon equal portions of meat sauce over each and sprinkle each with *2 tablespoons* (30 ml) cheese. Makes 8 Coney sandwiches.

^M*Microwave*

BURGER BUNDLES
Scrumptious . . . with a surprise stuffing.

450 g	1 lb. ground beef
	1 (6-oz./170 g) pkg. beef-flavored stuffing mix with wild rice
85 ml	⅓ cup milk
3 ml	½ teasp. salt
	1 (8-oz./226 g) can Hunt's Tomato Sauce
60 ml	¼ cup water
5 ml	1 teasp. Worcestershire
3 ml	½ teasp. rosemary

In bowl, combine beef, *½ cup* (125 ml) stuffing mix crumbs, milk and salt; mix well. Form into 6 thin 5-inch (13 cm) patties. Prepare *remaining* stuffing mix according to package directions. Mound equal portions in center of each meat patty; form patty into ball around stuffing and pinch edges to seal. Arrange in 7½- x 12- x 1½-inch (18 x 30 x 4 cm) baking dish; bake at 350° (175°C) 20 minutes; drain. Pour on Hunt's Sauce mixed with water, Worcestershire and rosemary; bake 15 minutes longer. Makes 4 to 6 servings.

HEARTY MEATBALL STEW
Meatballs make this stew super fast.

450 g	1 lb. ground beef
60 ml	¼ cup uncooked rice
60 ml	¼ cup grated Parmesan cheese
3 ml	½ teasp. garlic powder
	Salt
	2 (15-oz./425 g) cans Hunt's Tomato Sauce
15 ml	1 Tablesp. pure vegetable oil
	2 small onions, quartered
250 ml	1 cup sliced carrots
250 ml	1 cup sliced celery

Combine ground beef, rice, Parmesan, garlic powder and *1 teaspoon* (5 ml) salt with *¼ cup* (60 ml) Hunt's Sauce in medium mixing bowl. Form into 20 to 24 meatballs. In Dutch oven, lightly brown meatballs in oil. Drain fat. Add *remaining* Hunt's Sauce, *1 teaspoon* (5 ml) salt and remaining ingredients. Cover, simmer 30 minutes or until vegetables are done. Makes 4 to 6 servings.

Powdered or ground herbs and spices are more concentrated than the leaf, stick or seed form. Remember to use them sparingly.

New Ways To Serve Ground Beef

PIZZA HAMBURGER
A knife and fork pizza—meat makes the crust

450 g	1	lb. lean ground beef
60 ml	¼	cup minced green pepper
60 ml	¼	cup minced onion
5 ml	1	teasp. Worcestershire
5 ml	1	teasp. salt
1 ml	¼	teasp. pepper
	1	(8-oz./226 g) can Hunt's Tomato Sauce
250 ml	1	cup shredded mozzarella cheese
15 ml	1	Tablesp. chopped parsley
3 ml	½	teasp. basil
1 ml	¼	teasp. oregano

Combine first 6 ingredients; press against sides and bottom of 9-inch (23 cm) pie plate. Bake at 375° (190°C) 10 minutes; drain fat. Spread Hunt's Sauce over meat; top with remaining ingredients. Bake 10 minutes longer. Makes 4 servings.

New Ways To Serve Ground Beef

ALOHA BURGER STEAKS
Festive served Polynesian style with rice

675 g	1½	lbs. lean ground beef
60 ml	¼	cup finely chopped green pepper
	1	egg
5 ml	1	teasp. seasoned salt
	6	slices canned pineapple
	1	(8-oz./226 g) can Hunt's Tomato Sauce
15 ml	1	Tablesp. soy sauce
10 ml	2	teasp. brown sugar
10 ml	2	teasp. vinegar
3 ml	½	teasp. dry mustard

Combine beef, green pepper, egg and salt; shape into 6 patties. Press pineapple slice firmly into each patty. In skillet, brown quickly, pineapple side up; turn, brown pineapple side down. Drain fat, turn patties pineapple side up. Combine remaining ingredients, pour over patties. Simmer covered 5 to 10 minutes. Spoon extra sauce over servings. Makes 6 servings.

You can buy ground beef extended with soy protein in most markets. It is highly nutritious, shrinks less in cooking and costs less per pound.

COMPANY PATTY BROIL
Burgers topped with sour cream and cheese

	1 (8-oz./226 g) can Hunt's Tomato Sauce
30 ml	2 Tablesp. dry sherry or vinegar
30 ml	2 Tablesp. brown sugar
15 ml	1 Tablesp. prepared mustard
15 ml	1 Tablesp. Worcestershire
3 ml	½ teasp. salt
675 g	1½ lbs. lean ground beef
125 ml	½ cup crumbled cheese-flavor crackers
	1 egg
125 ml	½ cup sour cream with chives
85 ml	⅓ cup shredded Cheddar cheese

Combine Hunt's Sauce, sherry, brown sugar, mustard, Worcestershire and salt. Mix *¼ cup* (60 ml) of this mixture with beef, cracker crumbs and egg. Shape into 6 patties about 1 inch (3 cm) thick. Brush surfaces with sauce mixture. Broil 5 inches (13 cm) from heat 3 to 4 minutes. Turn, brush with *remaining* sauce; broil about 5 minutes longer. Top with sour cream and cheese. Makes 6 servings.

ORIENTAL BEEF RING
Meat loaf with a Far East accent

	1 (3-oz./84 g) can chow mein noodles
	1 (8-oz./226 g) can Hunt's Tomato Sauce with Onions
60 ml	¼ cup water
675 g	1½ lbs. lean ground beef
	1 egg
60 ml	¼ cup *each:* finely chopped green pepper and celery
45 ml	3 Tablesp. soy sauce
4 ml	¾ teasp. ground ginger
15 ml	1 Tablesp. brown sugar
	2 (7-oz./198 g) pkgs. frozen Chinese pea pods (snow peas), cooked
60 ml	¼ cup toasted slivered almonds
15 ml	1 Tablesp. butter or margarine

Crush *1 cup* (250 ml) noodles; reserve remainder. In bowl, combine crushed noodles, *¾ cup* (180 ml) Hunt's Sauce and water; let stand 5 minutes. Add beef, egg, green pepper, celery, *2 tablespoons* (30 ml) soy sauce and *¼ teaspoon* (1 ml) ginger; mix well. Pack into oiled 9-inch (23 cm) ring mold. Bake at 375° (190°C) 45 minutes. Pour off fat; invert on baking sheet. Bake 20 minutes longer, basting with mixture of brown sugar and *remaining* Hunt's Sauce, soy sauce and ginger. Arrange ring on platter; fill center with pea pods mixed with almonds, butter and remaining noodles. Makes 6 servings.

ALMOST LASAGNA
Takes half the work and it's economical, too

350 g	¾ lb. ground beef
	1 (15-oz./425 g) can Hunt's Tomato Herb Sauce
750 ml	3 cups water
225 g	8 ozs. narrow noodles
500 ml	2 cups cream style cottage cheese
30 ml	2 Tablesp. parsley flakes
5 ml	1 teasp. salt
5 ml	1 teasp. oregano
3 ml	½ teasp. garlic salt
	1 egg, slightly beaten
170 g	6 ozs. mozzarella cheese, shredded
60 ml	¼ cup grated Parmesan cheese

Brown beef in large pot; drain fat. Stir in Hunt's Sauce and water; bring to a boil. Add noodles and cook, covered, 5 to 7 minutes; stirring occasionally, until noodles are barely tender. In bowl, blend cottage cheese with next 5 ingredients. Grease a 7½- x 12- x 1½-inch (18 x 30 x 4 cm) baking dish. Fill with alternate layers of noodle mixture, cottage cheese filling and mozzarella cheese, ending with noodle mixture. Sprinkle with Parmesan cheese. Bake at 350° (175°C) 35 minutes; let stand 15 minutes before serving. Makes 6 to 8 servings.

MEDITERRANEAN PITA POCKETS^M
Arabic bread and sloppy joe filling

450 g	1 lb. ground beef
125 ml	½ cup chopped onion
60 ml	¼ cup minced celery
60 ml	¼ cup minced green pepper
	1 (15-oz./425 g) can Hunt's Tomato Herb Sauce
15 ml	1 Tablesp. lemon juice
5 ml	1 teasp. garlic powder
3 ml	½ teasp. seasoned salt
1 ml	¼ teasp. pepper
	6 small rounds pita or Arabic bread

Cook ground beef, onion, celery and green pepper together in a 10-inch (25 cm) skillet over medium heat until beef loses redness; drain fat. Stir in Hunt's Sauce, lemon juice and seasonings; simmer 5 minutes. Cut bread rounds in half crosswise. Use meat mixture to fill pockets that split open in bread halves. Makes 6 sandwiches.

M*Microwave*

Opposite: Mediterranean Pita Pockets

Hunt's Remarkable 7 Sauces

Tomato sauce, that handy ingredient on your pantry shelf, is said to be the seasoning used most often next to salt. And Hunt's gives you 7 remarkable ways to add the just right tomato sauce flavor to family or party fare.

There's Hunt's:

Tomato Sauce — subtly spiced and slowly simmered, this velvety smooth sauce is always dependable, ever versatile. (Your choice of) 8-, 15- and 29-oz. cans.

Tomato Sauce with Tomato Bits — juicy chunks of tomato pieces add personality plus to perfectly seasoned tomato sauce. 15-oz. can.

Tomato Sauce with Cheese — a robust but mellow tomato sauce seasoned with aged Romano cheese and selected spices. 8-oz. can.

Tomato Sauce with Mushrooms — the perfect blend of rich tomatoes, succulent pieces of mushrooms and spices for flavor flair. 8-oz. can.

Tomato Sauce with Onions — lightly seasoned but zesty with the wonderful flavor and texture of real chopped onions. 8-oz. can.

Tomato Herb Sauce — smooth homemade flavor of vine-ripened tomatoes simmered with onion, cheese, herbs and spices. 15-oz. can.

Tomato Sauce Special — tomato chunks, chopped onion, green bell peppers, celery and selected seasonings combined with delectable tomato sauce. Truly special. 15-oz. can.

And as remarkable as the flavors themselves: you can use any of Hunt's 7 Sauces in place of any tomato ingredient in most recipes.

When a recipe calls for:	You can use instead, Hunt's:
1 lb. fresh tomatoes, cooked	1 (8-oz.) can Tomato Sauce*
1 cup tomato puree	1 (8-oz.) can Tomato Sauce*
1 (1-lb.) can whole tomatoes	1 (15-oz.) can Tomato Sauce with Tomato Bits, plus ¼ cup water
1 (1-lb.) can stewed tomatoes	1 (15-oz.) can Tomato Sauce Special, plus ¼ cup water
1 (6-oz.) can tomato paste plus 1 cup water	1 (15-oz.) can Tomato Sauce*
Tomato Juice	Tomato sauce and water in equal amounts
1 (10¾-oz.) can tomato soup	1 (8-oz.) can Tomato Sauce* plus ¼ cup water

To add variety and enhance the flavor of all your tomato recipes, use any of Hunt's flavored tomato sauces in place of regular.

Index

Author/Hunt-Wesson Kitchens Staff:
Del Patterson, Martha Johnson, Carolyn Avelino,
Nancy Freeberg, Delois Brown
Design/Tom Hollingsworth
Design Direction/Doug Kennedy
Photography/Tom Kelley
Coordination/Pat Works